Political Philosophies & Nation-Building in Cameroon
Grounds for Remaking the Postcolony

Aseh Andrew

Langaa Research & Publishing CIG
Mankon, Bamenda

Publisher:
Langaa RPCIG
Langaa Research & Publishing Common Initiative Group
P.O. Box 902 Mankon
Bamenda
North West Region
Cameroon
Langaagrp@gmail.com
www.langaa-rpcig.net

Distributed in and outside N. America by African Books Collective
orders@africanbookscollective.com
www.africanbookscollective.com

ISBN: 978-9956-763-44-3

© Aseh Andrew 2016

All rights reserved.
No part of this book may be reproduced or transmitted in any form or by any means, mechanical or electronic, including photocopying and recording, or be stored in any information storage or retrieval system, without written permission from the publisher

Table of Contents

Acknowledgements.. v
Preface... vii
Corrigendum... xi
Definition of Concepts...................................... xiii

Chapter One
Fault Start at birthing a National facing
a historical challenge... 1

Chapter Two
Um Nyobe's Political Philosophy within
the UPC National Liberation Struggle................... 23

Chapter Three
Ahmadou Ahidjo's Political Ideas
for Nation-Building.. 45

Chapter Four
Paul Biya's New Deal Political Philosophy
for Nation-Building.. 75

Chapter Five
The lethargy of a post-colonial
Political Experiment1... 121

Chapter Six
The Pitfalls that thwarted the configuration
of a nation in Cameroon..................................... 163

Bibliography... 177

Acknowledgments

It is with a heart of appreciation that I acknowledge the contributions of the following: Prof. Jean Mfoulou, Prof. Chindji Kouleu Ferdinand, and Prof. Daniel Abwa, all of the Faculty of Arts, Letters and Social Sciences, University of Yaoundé 1, for their incisive comments after reading through the preliminary sketch of this work, part of which constituted the substance of what I presented at the Department of Sociology and Anthropology of the University of Yaoundé 1 in partial fulfilment of the requirement for the award of a Master's Degree in Political Sociology.

Preface

For quite some time now there has been a need for a comprehensive text on the function of thought in historical studies in general and the political sociology of Cameroon in particular. When the first edition of this book made its appearance in 2006 and proved to be an essential text for students pursuing studies in the historical sciences and political studies the exigency to revise it to bring out the role of thought in these sub disciplines became apparent.. This edition brings out how history is subject to political thought. To address this dynamic, the book delves into Sociology, Philosophy, Anthropology, Political Science, History, and even Economics which underpins bourgeoisie political thought. Bourgeoisie stands as a superordinate configuration and an externalised economic system. We see philosophy not in definitions but in its practical application - philosophy at work. The reader discovers how the "hidden hand of history" fashions a political thought which, in turn, creates its own history. What we see in the final analysis, instead of Cameroonians making history, history makes Cameroonians. It is a sad political story not only of how political ideas are fashioned in a post-colonial context but of how Europeans impose a superordinate arrangement on a people together with its philosophers.

We see, beginning in the 1950s, philosophers mandated by Europeans to "think the nation" on behalf of post-colonial subjects even on behalf of Cameroonians. "Thinking the nation" in Cameroon on behalf of Europeans, especially after the leaders of the national liberation struggle were all eliminated between 1958 and 1971, European philosophers put in place a "repressive machine" under which Cameroonians were subjected between 1958 and 1990. Repression gave way to a refined form of enslavement – a modernised version of slavery. Cameroonians joined the band wagon and have been producing and reproducing Western industrial economies while daydreaming of what they will never become. The whole idea of nation-building in post-colonial Africa is put in question.

Students of political studies will grapple with questions as to whether Cameroon is a state or a nation and questions of sovereignty and citizenship. The law that reproduces dominant relationships between Africa and Western industrial countries makes post-colonial subjugation possible. Because political philosophy nourishes its foundation, the treatment of these issues makes it obvious to the reader that political philosophy separate from its foundation. Political philosophy has deeply entrenched foundations in foreign sources. How that establishes an externalised and materialistic history; a history of foreign worship for material benefits. In turn material benefits invigorate foreign foundations and keeps oblivious Cameroonians slaving endlessly in attempts to attain a foreign objective. Thus slavery is sustained. While sustaining Cameroon does not stand on a home-grown philosophy but yields to an externalised historical process. Thus foreigners who are the dominant actors in the historical process determine a people's history. Citizens become passive participants. This bespeaks of a history of citizens bereft of thought acted upon by external forces charting the course of history. The direction of the lives of citizens as passive audience in the historical process must takes place, beyond their understanding. Call it mental slavery reproduced by the slaves themselves and kept alive by an understanding of the world imposed by post-colonial ideological contraptions.

Note to the reader. The reader will observe that as a study of political philosophy, facts of occurrence and dates have not been treated in greater detail. While the details of facts of occurrence and dates are important, the concern here has been with cause and effect. Therefore, the details of facts of occurrence and dates have been left for the historian. In other words, when I set out to write this book my intention was not to write the history of Cameroon but to sight the role of thought in historical studies. Hence, what you are about to read is not the historian's history but a theory of how history is a progression from motive to event. Then again, if we resorted to digging up the past; the intention was not to usurp the position of the historian. Digging up the past was done as a methodological prerequisite to show the processes through which political thought develops.

Aseh Andrew
2016

Corrigendum

Studies in the field of social anthropology have shown that Christianity was not properly introduced in Africa probably for racial reasons. In the first edition Aseh Andrew erroneously referred to Jesus Christ as "their Jesus Christ". Because of Adam's sin, a death sentence hangs over all humanity. As a good and loving father, God chose, preserved and protected the tribe of Israel to produce the Messiah to redeem humanity from that death sentence. When Jesus Christ died and resurrected on the third day, he expanded the boundaries of the blessings of Israel to include all humanity, especially those that acknowledge this truth and look up to him as Saviour. Jesus Christ is therefore, not Europe's Jesus Christ but the Saviour of the whole world. Jesus Christ is the Lord of lords and Saviour divinely preordained to come into the world through the tribe of Israel. Furthermore, Jesus Christ did not come to establish a religion but to free man from religion and to establish a new way by which man should relate with his creator and enjoy the fullness of life as a result of that relationship. Everything regarding this in the first edition not in line with these understandings stands withdrawn. The author deeply regrets any embarrassment statements in the first edition may have caused the children of God

Definitions of Concepts

Political Philosophy
Political philosophy is defined here as the product of political thought derived from the processes of the political 'imagining' of a nation. This means that political philosophy can take the form of a projection, a proposition, an idea, or a vision of society it seeks to create. In other words, political philosophy would refer to the power of imagining or of gestating, including all the contributions made within the structure to the process of giving political form to a transient social space in all its wholeness as a self-transformational totality.

Nation-Building
Nation-building is used in this book just as the philosophers of the Cameroon nation have used it – the realisation of what Benedict Anderson has described as an 'imagined community' (Anderson 1983: 15). Nation-building is therefore a post-colonial concept used to refer to a futile political activity that deals with what is seen only by the mind's eye.

Programme
A programme here is taken simply to mean a plan of action born out of the process of 'thinking' the nation, adopted or formulated to achieve the goal of national liberation with the major aim of building a nation with all its self-contained key structural characteristics which takes care of the human condition.

Strategy
A strategy is taken to denote the means or approach or better still the line of attack used to accomplish or inaugurate a political idea. We will look at the approaches by which the political philosophers of the nation in Cameroon intended to invent a

self-image that completely cast off the imperial yoke towards national liberation and the configuration of a momentary social space into a nation.

National Liberation Struggle

To liberate means to set free and to engage in a national liberation struggle. It means to struggle to free one's national territory from all the eccentricities of foreign interventions that hinder its people from their fundamental freedom to self-determination within the framework of a nation. The national liberation struggle is also an intellectual activity which seeks to liberate political philosophy from the schema of master narratives with the intention to clear the stage for the rethinking of a nation whose foundation philosophy and its legitimate basis of existence is not subject to a foreign source of influence.

Chapter One

The Fault Starts at Birthing a Nation facing a Historical Challenge

The ability of a people to reclaim what they have lost and to establish a nation depends principally on their capacity to master the historical context in which they base thought and action. This chapter scrutinizes the response of Cameroonians to a historical challenge that confronted and obliged them to overcome as a prerequisite to birthing a nation. After accentuating the line of attack by which Cameroonians undertook birthing a nation a picture of emerges that Cameroonians don't seem to have mastered the historical context in which they based thought and action

Before we delve into the heart of the matter, note that prior to the Berlin Conference of 1884 in which the invasion, rape and destruction of the land and peoples of Africa by Europeans was formalised, Cameroon did not exist as a nation. The area today called Cameroon was inhabited by interdependent self-governing ethno-political entities or pre-modern nations, which shared similarity and difference. Before this formalized invasion and dehumanisation of its peoples, European pirates, beginning with the Portuguese, made rounds in the Atlantic coastline of West Africa in mid-1772, spied on the peoples and monitored their chattels and reactions to intrusions. After the Berlin Conference, Germans 'officially' invaded from 1884 to 1916 with a mission to enslave its people in order to build up an ailing German economy. The Germans raped it under the appellation *Kamerun*, a German derivative from the original Portuguese appellation of *Cameroes*, meaning prawns or crabs.

In 1916 the allied troops of France and Britain, in the course of World War I, seized the territory from the Germans and shared it amongst themselves. France took three-quarters and

Britain the rest. The Treaty of Marseille formalized this arrangement. After the Anglo-France allied forces defeated the Germans, the French and British introduced the new appellations of Cameroun and Cameroon respectively. They targeted the territory to growing their economies under the aegis of the League of Nations as mandated territories and later under the United Nations as trust territories (Konde 1998: 10-11; Ngoh 2004:1). Historian Richard Joseph recalls Cameroon was brought within the French Empire during the course of World War I after the pattern of colonial administration had already been established in West and Equatorial Africa. The pattern of colonial administration now extended to the former German territory with only minor changes to satisfy the League of Nations. Unlike British involvement in West Africa, where the metropole usually let trading companies undertake the task of subjugation and administration, France during the last two decades of the 19th century, committed to a policy of military conquest in the Western Sudan (Joseph 1978: 7).

As a result of the French military conquest of its mandated territory during this period and the British system of indirect exploitation of its own fraction, the route to Cameroon becoming a "nation-state", a project that was initiated immediately after World War II upon the inception of the *Union des populations du Cameroun* (UPC), seem to have occurred in a context of changing perceptions that had already hampered political thinking. This was made worst by ethnic and political fragmentation orchestrated by the very Western invading forces as a political strategy to maintain dominance. The UPC national liberation movement, born in the French occupied territory on April 10, 1948 as a response to the general quest for freedom from European throttlehold on conquered peoples found itself the lone voice in the midst of a multiplicity of political formations. Most of these formations had self-seeking agendas with no intention to develop a home-grown political philosophy on which the new nation would stand.H0wever, post-war reforms gave a ray of hope for peace that never came to fruition.

Infractions came to characterise post-war political thinking in Cameroon. The political sphere reflected these troubles as individuals and the socio-political formations. These parties did not present any real nationalist agendas but rather sought to use the ray of hope offered by the post-war settlement reform to benefit from what they seem to have perceived as the spin-offs of the European invasion of Africa.

Individuals and the socio-political formations seem to have been convinced that by associating politically with and defining their own political agendas within the European global economic exploitation and political domination they would achieve peace and freedom. With the exception of the UPC, political parties on both sides of the colonially engineered linguistic divide did the same thing: seek improvement of conditions from European assailants instead of rallying political forces to drive them away. Parties sought to rearrange the social space to achieve political form based on a self-imposed political philosophy derived from and deeply rooted in the consciousness of the people.

As early as 1939 the Cameroon Welfare Union (CWU) saw the light of day in the British occupied territory. CWU emerged from a Bakweri ethnic association. Its mission was not that of anti-European invasion. Characteristic of the political behaviour of 'improvement on condition' that prevailed the CWU later on remodelled its ideals to include demands for representation of the people of the British territory of Cameroon known in the Nigerian Legislative Council in Lagos as Southern Cameroons. Between 1940 and 1959 political formations proliferated in the Southern Cameroons. Others such as the CPNC of Dr. E.M.L Endeley, sought improvement in the conditions of Southern Cameroonians in the Nigerian political set-up. Others, such as the pro-reunification KNDP of J.N. Foncha, were created under the same conditions that led to the creation of the UPC in the French occupied territory. These conditions characterized the dissatisfaction with the European invasion, degradation, and dehumanisation of the people as Ebune (1992: 143) recalls.

These groups sought political autonomy of an independent Southern Cameroons.

Close examination of the activities of political parties in the British occupied territory of Cameroon reveals that none of the political parties in West Cameroon took a stand against European invasion, degradation, and dehumanisation and none of them had a clear cut national agenda, except perhaps the Bakweri Land Committee, an ethnic formation that has been fighting since colonial times to retrieve the stolen land of the Bakweri people. Worst still, none of the political parties in the then West Cameroon concerned themselves with birthing a nation with a genuine non-foreign philosophy within the appellation Cameroon. Parties having emerged from ethnic associations, which Ebune says were "unstable and short-lived, confused in their aims ... [they rather became useful] as informal arms of the [British colonial] administration" Ebune (1992: 111, 112). Supported by the British invaders themselves, political parties in West Cameroon were seeking improvement in conditions from the same Europeans they were supposed to have opposed. Their individual approaches diverged on the question of the personality of the British invaded territory. They based arguments within the logic of co-operation with European invaders. Thus they generally lacked the virulent and radical vision in approach to the Cameroon national problem. That problem was that Cameroon remained under foreign occupation. The UPC, however, aptly articulated this problem.

Nevertheless, in 1948, under the umbrella of French Cameroon Welfare Union (FCWU), was organised by some East Cameroonians who had fled from forced labour and forced military service in East Cameroon during the pre- and post-World War II era into Southern Cameroons FCWU's Dr. Endeley strongly supported the idea of the reunification of the two halves of Cameroon, part of the solution to the problem. In 1949 Dr. Endeley, who had shown open dissatisfaction with British invasion and destruction of their occupied portion of Cameroon, founded the Cameroon National Federation (CNF).

Reunification was on the CNF agenda. In that same year in an address to the UN Visiting Mission to Cameroon he held the British invaders responsible for appalling conditions of people of West Cameroon under Nigeria. Dibongue Jabea, one of the East Cameroonians fled into the Southern Cameroons and created the Kamerun United National Congress (KUNC) in 1951, with reunification on its agenda also. Dr. Endeley identified with KUNC and became its Vice President.

Reunification was getting popular due to the invasion of the Southern Cameroons by the Ibos of Nigeria, their contemptuous economic practices and with Dr. Endeley's ties with the UPC. These events led to the further fragmentation by the administration of West Cameroon into the North West and South West provinces. This administrative move probably aimed to avert the spread of national consciousness inherent in the UPC political agenda. Surprisingly Dr. Endeley, in 1954, publicly denounced his reunification stand and ties with the UPC in support of continues ties with Nigeria. UPC was feared to be a communist party. Dr. Endeley's actions precipitated a split in his party, the Kamerun National Congress (KNC) with J. N. Foncha and A. N. Jua leaving to form the Kamerun National Democratic Party (KNDP). The KNDP maintained the reunification stand. This stand seems to have gathered some popularity in the Southern Cameroons where it was first mooted in 1948.

N.N. Mbile's Kamerun People's Party (KPP) merged with Dr. Endeley's KNC in 1957 to become the Cameroon People's National Congress (CPNC). This alliance strongly supporting integration with Nigeria. On the other hand, KNDP, under J.N. Foncha as its president, campaigned on the reunification platform and won 16 out of the 24 seats in the January 1959 election. He eventually became the first Prime Minister of West Cameroon not because he had an agenda to give Cameroonians the opportunity to reorder themselves into a political form but because he was a participant in the mistreatment that Europeans were wreaking on Cameroonians.

When reunification was finally achieved in 1961, through an election that seems to have been intentionally designed by the UN to be confusing, the Fumban Conference sat down in July of that year to draw a Charter for the new Federation. Unfortunately, Ahmadou Ahidjo, Cameroon's first president, who also did not demonstrate any genuine nationalist thinking single-handedly abrogated it and extended the French engineered state-of-emergency rule to include West Cameroon.

In East Cameroon, other political parties besides the UPC existed as well. But unlike the UPC none were revolutionary nor rooted in political thinking against the invasion by foreigners. Rather, the political parties in East Cameroon existed in a kind of a convivial relationship with French oppressors. In 1946 the Representative Assembly of French Cameroon (ARCAM) was established. Ostensibly the French, Soppo Priso, established ARCAM had also created JEUCAFRA (*Jeunesse camerounais française*). Soppo Priso quickly became its president even after it was transformed into ATCAM (*Assemblée Territoriale Camerounais*). The composition of the Assembly comprised of 40 deputies; 16 French Nationals and 24 Cameroonians. They were elected into ATCAM through a franchise that was selected mainly from the budding "elite" category. This was also the same criterion that was used in selecting those who qualified to be deputies under ARCAM. This indicates that political thinking in post-war Cameroon in general was about collaboration with the European invaders. Although those who constituted ARCAM did not form political parties, during the 1952 election when ARCAM had become ATCAM, the set-up did not change very much. The composition of the chamber only changed in that the number of Cameroonians in it had increased from 24 to 32 while that of French nationals dropped to 18. This turn of events can be interpreted as an indication that the French were gradually handing over their reign in Cameroon to "natives" who were to remain a close collaborating stratum. Among the Cameroonians "elected" was Charles Okala who, as a member of ATCAM and Senator in the French Council, addressed the UN Fourth

Committee charging the French with human abuses in Cameroon. This charge was upheld and articulated by Um Nyobe before the same UN Fourth Committee. It was at this time that Um Nyobe's concern about the need to reunify the two halves of Cameroon heretofore ripped apart by European criminal practices gained some momentum.

Otherwise, almost all the political formations that existed in East Cameroon, except the UPC, were intractably linked to the French. All political leaders in that region of Cameroon grew from amongst the ranks of the French occupation. This gave rise to the notion among them that they were part of the 'greater France' who must speak only the French language and see France as 'home'. Hence, their major concern was not with birthing a nation under the appellation Cameroon detached from that of France. Even Soppo Priso, for example, who claimed to be the opposition, was the president of an Assembly created and controlled by France, obeying orders that were passed by the French through it.

Amongst other political parties in East Cameroon that were not detached from France, was the *Bloc Démocratique Camerounais* (BDC) of Dr. Louis-Paul Aujoulat, a French man and a Roman Catholic medical doctor. BDC played a determinant role in the political life of Cameroon modelling political thinking of those on whom the French were to hand Cameroon's destiny. The BDC, which was created in 1951, died in 1956 after a short but decisive hex of existence. As a floating political party, made up mainly of civil servants, chiefs, and "elites", its organisation and political agenda was similar to that of the UPC. However, BDC hid an agenda of maintaining French dominance over Cameroonians as Zang-Atangana (1989: 179) puts it. Since in 1952 the reunification issue was already on the public agenda, having spread through the UPC from Southern Cameroons where it originated, the BDC was prompted to take a stand in favour of reunification at its congress in 1953. Ahmadou Ahidjo, who was politically groomed within the ranks of the BDC was also to adopt the programme of this fake nationalist party while in office, first as Prime Minister of East Cameroon in 1958. Ahidjo, as Head of State, epitomised this charade by the 1972 'quiet revolution' which was part of the BDC political agenda The BDC political agenda groomed Ahmadou Ahidjo.

The growth of political parties in the three segments of Cameroon were instrumental in bringing certain individuals into prominence. However, this flourishing of political parties only helped to confuse the political scene and retarded the growth of political consciousness. Political parties on both sides of the divide including even Northern Cameroon that was lost to Nigeria failed to rally forces against the invasion of Europeans and stymied the development of a purely original nationalist idea. Such an idea would have guided the process of Cameroon nation building.

In East Cameroon this was the case with the likes of BDC, ARCAM, JEUCAFRA, etc. In the Southern Cameroons the invading British encouraged multi-party politics since this reduced political action to mere political debates. In the Northern territory of Cameroon, lost to Nigeria, involvement of non-indigenes in the formation of political parties such as the Northern People's Congress (NPC) and the Northern Elements Progressive Union (NEPU), created a confusion about the future of the Northern Cameroons. This gave the imperial UN and the British the opportunity to organise a plebiscite to decide the fate of that part of Cameroon (Ngoh 2004: 3). This confirms the hypothesis that the history of political parties on both sides of the territory did not demonstrate an intention to create a nation under the appellation Cameroon. Such an intention would have yielded a process that would have included the recapturing of the lost totality of the colonised subjects and then would have reconfigured the social space into a nation in which citizens would have had the possibility to effectively defining their lives by themselves.

The fact that not only did Europeans take central stage in directing the political activities in the territory but also by the fact that Cameroonians, to a certain degree, seemed to have been confused at the decisive moment -- the moment they had to state categorically their claim to what they had lost. Instead the lure and grandeur of political parties titillated and enthralled them. Today the leaders of such political parties are considered as national heroes not because of any national agenda they carried out but simply because they created political parties that enabled them to participate in the enterprise of evil. The whole political process, from the onset, when not triggered by Europeans, most often received their benediction. The UN, for its part, did not prove the neutral arbiter it is often misunderstood to be. Rather it availed itself as an institution out to foster the mistreatment of blacks by whites. This role can be considered international terrorism rather than the guarantor of world peace for which it was created. For example, instead of telling Britain, then in possession of the vast land stolen by the Germans from the Bakweri people who had made several petitions to the UN since August 12, 1946, "please hand back the land to its rightful owners" the UN gave the British the upper hand. The UN did this by permitting the British to argue their case justifying why they must rob the Bakweri of their land in the cause of which the British encouraged the emergence of alternative sheds of opinion to rival the Bakweri Land Committee.

Eventually, in collusion with the UN Trusteeship Council Britain came up with a brainwashing programme they called the Man O' War Bay Scheme to indoctrinate Bakweri youths in what they called "character training." Character training was intended to soften the Bakweri youths to make them more yielding to the British mission of invasion and occupation than those they described as the "less educated" (see Ngoh 2004: 19-26). This illustrates how the UN confused issues on the international scene in a way that made self-determination difficult to achieve. If the UN served as a neutral arbiter it would not have classified peoples of the world into two simplistic categories, namely, the superior and the inferior and then proceeded to "mandate" the superior ones to raise the inferior ones up to the standards of "humanity". The "trusted" people of the UN maltreated and still maltreat and enslave those the UN inadvertently considered to be inferior.

Sadly, Cameroonians generally saw the creation of political parties as a means through which they could rub shoulders with the white man. Even today that mentality remains quite unchanged. Themes such as national liberation and nation-building which animated political life in Cameroon in the 1950s seem to have originated and ended with the UPC in 1971. Nobody talks about national liberation and nation-building anymore, probably because the Europeans enslavers and exploiters have largely vacated. The prevailing themes that animate political life in Cameroon today centre around democracy and the equitable distribution of resources out of which arose Ahmadou Ahidjo's politics of regional balancing. With such themes governing the mental life of Cameroonians, political parties created today focus on democracy and the equitable distribution of national wealth., This means that in the political thinking of Cameroonians, Cameroon as a place to live in and share in the benefits of what the structure has to offer had already emerged. This notion of an existing Cameroon prevails irrespective of what kind of structure it is and irrespective of how it emerged. From the onset Cameroonians commonly wished to see this happen because as we saw above, political parties that cropped up in the two divided sections of the territory shared the perspective that carried no nationalist agenda. Even as early as in 1955 when Soppo Priso, who was an initial member of the UPC, formed the MACNA (*Mouvement d'action national*), which evolved into *Action National*, it made no input on the nationalist agenda. Yet a nationalist agenda was supposed to have been characteristic of the post-war political thinking in all colonised territories. MACNA or *Action National* did not fill the political vacuum that was created by the banning of the UPC by the French either. André-Marie Mbida, who had also militated in the UPC before leaving to form the PDC, did not make a difference on the political scene either, his political party did not have a political agenda that signalled the exigency of the day, which was freedom from colonial rule and nation-building. It should be recalled that André-Marie Mbida left the UPC and flirted with the BDC before forming the PDC. The PDC created no earth tremors either although Mbida turned around to be a nonconformist against the wishes of the French when they enthroned him as the first Prime Minister of East Cameroon in 1957.

Among all the many political formations that existed in the eastern part of the territory or in the territory as a whole, only the UPC maintained its identity as the lone dominant political force against the mistreatment of blacks by whites, and maintained its revolutionary moral fibre, with a clear cut nationalist agenda rooted in the anti-European occupation of Cameroon. The UPC was a well organised political formation under the leadership of Um Nyobe, its Secretary General.

Unfortunately, in its dogged struggle against the European forces (1916–1961), the UPC national liberation movement, which had a broad national intention, was systematically suppressed and destroyed by the French with local support from their local collaborators as Mbembe (1984: 28) points out. The uninspiring mentality that permeated the political scene throughout the entire territory. A vacuum was created that no political party could readily fill following the banning of the UPC in 1955. Not even the PDC of André-Marie Mbida who had militated in the UPC before forming it, could fill the vacuum left by the banning of the UPC. However, The UPC remained determined to uphold its ideals. The UPC realized that the vacuum created by its banning could not be filled. The UPC took a more revolutionary tact in favour of immediate independence instead. Regrettably, a death sentence was passed on the first national liberation struggle in Cameroon after its Secretary General and inspirational leader, Um Nyobe, was killed in September 13, 1958 in the forest near the present day Sanaga Maritime division. The French secret agents (*Main Rouge*) poisoned to death Its President, Dr. Felix Roland Moumié, by in Geneva in 1960. Thus by 1960, a death sentence passed on the first national liberation struggle in Cameroon as no political party either in the eastern flank or in the western flank of the territory could step into the shoes of the UPC. This same uninspiring mentality permeated the political scene throughout Cameroon leading to the systematic killing of its president who could have carried the flame of the liberation struggle after the death of Um Nyobe. Europeans, whether French or British shared a common colonial purpose against the colonised subjects. For that reason, the wishes of the French were upheld by the British and vice versa. Nobody could escape from the French occupied section of the territory and take refuge in the British occupied section either. Their common interest was to subject, exploit and possibly kill Africans for the growth and expansion of the European economy. Dr. Felix Roland Moumié's exile in Geneva where he sought refuge in vain after the declaration of war on the Cameroon people by France was prompted by his deportation from Southern Cameroon by the British Governor General of Nigeria who ruled over that portion of Cameroon at the time. Its last guerrilla leader, Ernest Ouandié, was finally killed by a public firing squad in Bafoussam in 1971 at the command of the local collaborators (Mukong 1985: 23; Joseph 1974: 430, 432, 438). Meanwhile, at the peak of the UPC guerrilla struggle for freedom took a more revolutionary dimension immediately after Um Nyobe was killed. After having concocted a conservative north/south alliance to balance the powers of the UPC, it was then time for France to hand over the command baton to the local collaborators to continue with the relay. At that point, the economic survival and global expansion of the European global pirates took a local colour. Consequently,

"On 9 May 1957, the Cameroon State under Trusteeship came into existence. Andre-Marie Mbida was appointed by [the French] High Commissioner Pierre Messmer to head the first Cameroon Government ... In February 1958, the recently-appointed Governor, Jean Remadier, engineered the replacement of Mbida by the Northerner Ahmadou Ahidjo a man notable until then for the little impact he had made in Cameron politics, or as a representative in Paris. The way was now clear for the granting of independence [to East Cameroon] on 1 January 1960 to the very forces in the country which had most opposed the struggle for independence during the previous fifteen years" (Joseph 1974: 438, 440).

When the Europeans thus receded to the background and handed the country to local collaborators, it became evident that Cameroon was on no path to becoming a nation as its efforts had a foreign foundation philosophy. Cameroon was piloted by an indigenous elite. Yet, Cameroonians were ipso factor disengaged from the process of birthing a nation for themselves by themselves. History had played tricks on Cameroonians. Consequently, the path it took was not that of birthing a nation from the pre-existing ones but to co-opt its people as 'obedient servants' of Europeans. Cameroonians became as slavish imitators of the European people based on European-engineered development plans which benefitted Europeans rather than Cameroonians. Cameroonians were left oblivious implementers of such development plans. After the baton of command was passed to local collaborators, Cameroon then emerged in history as a replica, a copy or better still a caricature of the European model. This also led to the assimilation of the British territory of Cameroon following a vociferous referendum of May 20, 1972 that abolished the federal structure put in place after the October 1, 1961 plebiscite after which Cameroon lost part of its northern territory to Nigeria. In other words, that chain of events established an impromptu state by the French and their local allies with a state of emergency as the basis of government. Under this state of affairs West Cameroon was swallowed up by East Cameroun on whom France had imposed a conditional independence on January 1, 1960.

This historical sequence of events, orchestrated and realised by Europeans, ushered into existence a political entity that has come to be known as Cameroon. Cameroonians struggle to define their lives within it without asking how it happened. If truth be told, this sequence of events quenched the national liberation flames and so ended the UPC dream of national independence, reunification, and nation-building (c.f. Bayart 1980: 159). The end of the UPC dream of national independence, reunification, and nation-building ushered in Cameroon and Cameroonians into a new dawn, a new dawn characterised by the triumph of new political actors on the national scene with new ideas and new approaches to nationalism and nation-building. Unfortunately, these new political actors acted in response to the wishes of the Europeans who continued to control the structure from the background through them. In other words, the triumph of these new political actors on the national scene otherwise known as the "governing "elite" were French-made and were intended to be used as puppets for Frances assimilation policy (Mukong 1985: 7). The rising wave of nationalism in the colonies at its peak between 1956 and 1958 required the French policy of assimilation. Hence, the French policy of assimilation was intended to serve as a counter strategy to the rising wave of nationalism in the colonies. The political destiny of Cameroon was handed to people in whose trapped mind set the path for the thinking of the nation was a foregone conclusion. European "master thinkers" "gave" them the mandate and had already laid the foundation for the take-off of what was to emerge in Cameroon as a power structure. As collaborators in the European enslavement, therefore, they saw nothing wrong when France, like God, made Cameroon in its own image or likeness.

Furthermore, in 1966 all the political parties in Cameroon were fused into one political party, the CNU of Ahmadou Ahidjo. That achieved nothing else but gave Ahmadou Ahidjo the power to effectively represent European interests in Cameroon unopposed. The suppression of freedom of speech as well as the suppression of all forms of association reinforced this unmediated representation. In other words, the suppression of freedom of speech and the suppression of all forms of association silenced the voices of Cameroonians and made

Ahmadou Ahidjo the only cock that could crow in Cameroon. The UN ratified it since it "recognised" what France and Britain had concocted and put in place here as a country between 1960 and 1961. That ratification actually proved a rallying instrument through which France could control political thinking in Cameroon. To ensure that Ahmadou Ahidjo had total control of the entire territory on behalf of France, in 1961 West Cameroon was roped in. The British left having played a dubious role in laying a rickety foundation for the region it raped, looted and destroyed. Ahmadou Ahidjo emerged victorious as France's best choice, based on ethnic considerations. Ahidjo was to head the second indigenous East Cameroon administration barely nine months after the collapse of the first under the tutelage, support and counsel of the French authorities. (Zang-Atangana 1989: 101). He pledged his unremitting collaboration with France to continue enslaving the people of Cameroon to the best interest of France.

This followed de Gaulle's imposition in 1958 of two alternatives on the West Africans and particularity those of the Equatorial sub region. The alternatives compelled them to either gain "autonomy within the *communauté* in which France would clearly control the economic levers, or independence – which was a polite term for expulsion into a franc less world. (Calvocoressi 1985: 345). Confused, Ahmadou Ahidjo, like his other African counterparts, except Sekou Touré of Guinea who said no, opted for the former. Through this alternative Cameroon gained its status as a "French possession" alongside the Southern territory which was clandestinely grafted into the union by Ahidjo. West Cameroon's union with the French concocted machinery can be said to have been a clandestine grafting because in 1972 Ahmadou Ahidjo single-handedly abolished the 1961 concocted federal structure. What Ahmadou Ahidjo began in 1972 was completed in 1984 by Paul Biya. All of these machinations fell in line with the fact that;

"French decolonisation was far less genuinely a retreat from Africa than its British equivalent. In part, it was a nominal change of sovereignty that did not much affect basic French interests. On achieving independence, the new nations signed agreements with France on foreign aid and defence that reinforced French cultural and economic predominance and left the French army as guarantor of the new regime" (Freund 1984: 226, 227).

This makes it clear that French decolonisation was in fact more a tactful retreat from the scene than the expression of a genuine willingness to physically pack bag and baggage and leave. Ahmadou Ahidjo became the first President of the French trusteeship territory of Cameroon in 1960 as a French protégée, and the first president of the Federal Republic of Cameroon in 1961, and then the President of the unitary state from 1972 to 1982. As Ndiva Kofele-Kale (1980) shows us, with no political agenda according to Mukong (1985: 8), Ahidjo launched his nation-building project under the banner of national unity and regional balance, meaning that he had intended to bring Cameroonians together for the equitable sharing of what the French concocted arrangement had to offer. Unfortunately for Cameroonians that is exactly what Ahmadou Ahidjo's concept of national unity and regional balance meant; at least that is what it looked like. The basic concepts of Ahmadou Ahidjo's political agenda was laid down by Um Nyobe within the framework of the UPC national liberation struggle as part of the nationalist project, which included the mobilisation of revolutionary forces against European invasion towards national independence. This UPC agenda which was later on embodied in the UPC strategy of independence before reunification was later on copied by the European mandated political philosophers. So we see that Ahmadou Ahidjo's concept of national unity and regional balance was a twisted copy of the UPC agenda. Furthermore, Paul Biya, like his predecessor, who could lay little or no claim to a national mandate at the time of his accession to power as

Joseph (1978: 3) observes also tried to remodel the UPC agenda. Both men did so as a political strategy to give themselves a veneer of legitimacy among Cameroonians. To paraphrase Mbembe (1984: 108); Joseph (ibid) and Bayart (ibid), the aim of these European mandated political philosophers was just to make Cameroonians belief that they too have a nation-building and national development agenda. Ebune (1992: 141) observes that even the Kamerun National Democratic Party (KNDP), following its creation in 1955 by J. N Foncha also upheld the UPC agenda though with a soft approach to national liberation. Unfortunately, President Ahmadou Ahidjo, who falls in the category of those whom Aina calls "agents of international institutions and donor organisations" (Aina 2003: 84), and not a nationalist, since "he could lay little claim to a national mandate at the time of his accession to power according to Joseph (1978: 3), subverted it.

Consequently, the UPC agenda's application turned out to achieve the exact opposite of what it was originally intended to achieve (Kengne Pokam 1986:56; Joseph 1978: 126) especially, as Ahmadou Ahidjo's metropolitan patrons or foreign partners set the agenda thus determining from the backstage what they intended to achieve in Cameroon (Clignet 1980: 330; Joseph ibid: 29). The investment code of June 27, 1960 and other forms of manipulative legislation completed the process of French assimilation giving the French leeway to manipulate political outcomes in Cameroon Besides the investment code of June 27, 1960, accords and development agendas also proved useful in subjecting the country to the destructive practices of metropolitan capital (Joseph 1878: 133; Ndongko 1980: 246; Ngwasiri 1997: 41). President Paul Biya succeeded Ahidjo in 1982 in an uneventful manner, without any transition in what Tobie-Kuoh (1992: 18) describes as a typical ancient Roman style. The provisions of the 1979 modified constitution (Ngayap 1983: 7), reformulated the original UPC political agenda to include the concept of national integration (Biya 1986: 30). Even this turned out to achieve the opposite of unity.

Consequently, for over half a century today after the French foisted their local collaborators on Cameroon under the guise of what Cameroonians were made to belief that it was independence, and over sixty years after the national liberation project was launched, a fractured and contested public sphere that selectively "favours" certain social categories for the success of the project of domination governs Cameroon (Nfamewih Aseh 2011). The goal of the national liberation project was to enable Cameroonians to reclaim what they have lost. They never did and that is still far from being a reality today (Kengne Pokam 1986:18) Cameroon could only have emerged in history as a country with a fractured and contested public sphere that selectively gives special treatment to certain social categories for the success of the project of domination. This unfortunate turn of events can very easily be understood as a direct consequence of the killing of the nationalist leaders and the total destruction of the national liberation movement. Fondo Sikod (1997) maintains that both President Ahmadou Ahidjo's economic policy of planned liberalism and President Paul Biya's New Deal doctrine engraved in his political philosophy of communal liberalism have failed to achieve the goal of freedom, national integration and political unity through resource allocation. Joseph (1978: 129-130) articulates the view that this failure can be explained by "the archaic structures of exploitation implanted by the direct colonial regime[Were]simply adapted to the new juridical situation created by the proclamation of formal independence without any transformation or re-adaptation to the pre-existing social and political reality" (Joseph 1978: 129-130).

Seen through a different lens, the revolutionary idea in the struggle for freedom, independence and nation-building in Cameroon ignited by the post-World War II reforms, epitomised by the UPC under Um Nyobe, was destroyed by the European invaders who established their puppets instead to implement their programmes. An official capacity couldn't have been a panacea to the cries of Cameroonians for freedom.

Furthermore, in spite of the change of guards in 1982, which was just an inheritance of the same obsolete structures (Ngayap ibid and Ntumazah 2001) , no genuine will has prevailed to establish a harmonious, socio-culturally integrated, economically and politically independent, united and powerful nation free from external hegemonic influences(Konings and Nyamnjoh 2003: 8; Kengne Pokam 1986: 17).

Although the local collaborators pretended to have been pre-occupied with nation-building in the 1960s and 1970s by putting forward agendas that bore a semblance of national unity and socio-economic development, a subversion of the national liberation programme, the fruits of which were to be shared among the various regions in a fashion that will keep the nation at equilibrium, the reality on the ground in terms of goal attainment was totally different. A set of general or broad based principles for nationhood failed to emerge. These principles would have reflected the socio-economic reality , determined a unique political system and outlined its institutions and establish how common efforts, interests, techniques, concepts, beliefs, attitudes and purposes would flow together to achieve the goal of freedom and nation-building in consonant with the social weave and texture of Cameroon(Bayart 1980:162)., Cameroon remained a collection of social aggregates only. Even the liberalisation agendas of the late 1980s, spanning the 1990s into the 2000s only worsened the situation. Cameroon did not seize opportunities to become more that a mere collection of social aggregates.

Within this context Cameroon's narrow non-productive privileged elite emerged at the middle and upper echelons of the state. (Bayart 1978: 66; Lippens and Joseph 1978: 111; Ngayap 1983: 21; Kengne Pokam 1986: 57-70). Before the elaboration of Cameroon vision 2035 by President Paul Biya, only the few disjunctive urban configurations that were spawned into existence at the peripheries of the pre-existing self-governing ethno-political entities by European economic rapacious activities, a few kilometres of tarred roads plus those that were achieved under the famous five year development plans of the 1960s and 1970s, with the annual growth rate of nearly 7 percent of the 1970s, and projects realised through bilateral corporations, were used as indicators of the progress made in the nation-building project (Johnson in Foreword to Ndiva Kofele-Kale 1980: XVII). Within the framework of President Ahmadou Ahidjo's politics of regional balance:

> "Regional power conflicts were suppressed by incorporating all the large ethnic-regional power blocks into the state organisation, in exchange of strict loyalty to the state. This created regional hegemonies, which disfavoured other groups and resulted in imbalances within the regions (provinces)" (Adri van den Berg 1997: 165).

The reintroduction of multi-party polities in Cameroon in the 1990s, under President Paul Biya ushered in an air of freedom. These polities also destroyed Cameroon's economic structural base of European origins. Regional imbalances re-emerged. Ethnic groups were politically and economically marginalised and forgotten within the "prebendal state". (Jean-Francois Medard [add citation]) Contrary opinions suppressed under the state of emergency legislation (Joseph 1978: 203) resurfaced and expressed in diverse forms, demanding a just share of the benefits Cameroon offers. The therapy of liberalisation and privatisation, were part of the Structural Adjustment Plan (SAP) of the late 1980s and 1990s. Prescribed by the World Bank/IMF the SAP replaced the Five Year Development Plans, and the Poverty Reduction Strategy Paper (PRSP) of the 2000s. The HIPC initiative and the struggle to reach the IMF completion point target, spawned levels of poverty the scale of which wrought damaging consequences on human lives never known before.

In the course of these transitions, Cameroonians have known only moral deficiency, human suffering, and the looting of their material wealth, a constant reduction in income, hikes in commodity prices, and a heavy taxation burden. These deprivations and corruptions enables the vermin in power to carry on criminal activities in collusion with the metropolitan powers which are fronted by international financial institutions such as the IMF/World Bank. Liberalisation only resulted in ethnic and regional tensions and divisions and the social unrests that marked the Biya regime in the 1990s (Fogui 1990: 56; Nyamnjoh 1999: 101). This state of affairs characterised the post-colonial state in Cameroon. This state of affairs conforms to the theory of economic and psychological degradation of imperialism analysed by Frantz Fanon (1967). It also agrees with the theory of Europe's rape and underdevelopment of Africa eloquently elaborated by Walter Rodney (1972). It also clearly indicates that nation-building in Cameroon kicked off on a bad footing, especially after the destruction of the national liberation movement with the assistance of those whose intention was not to establish a nation in Cameroon with its own identity, free from foreign influences.

Identity grows from a sense of sameness among people who act as a corporate group. Together this group creates social structures within which they ensure the persistence of an autonomous, self-generating social pattern. Their effort achieves a tradition of continuity in the production and reproduction of the self. Political actors in post-colonial Cameroon seem to have been obsessed rather with the post-colonial theory of state formation. They forgot to arm themselves with an inimitable linguistic and cultural capital in their struggle to give Cameroonians the possibility to forge an identity. These politicians failed to devise methods of ensuring the permanence of that self-image with room for innovative behaviour within the identity group. These methods would have forged a nation. They hoped by participation in a political process set afoot by foreigners to draw benefits from it. This participation has rather produced a hybridised Cameroonian identity in which the Cameroonian people are a caricature of the West. They are neither themselves nor Westerners and Cameroon itself not a nation with a unique culture and identity. Instead the culture and identity has become a derivation from a process of composition, decomposition and the recomposition of the pre-existing ones. This presents a perplexing situation. An appropriate analysis of Cameroonian political life within the post-colonial context, especially after the destruction of the national liberation movement could explain this effect. An appropriate analysis would highlight what this has come to mean for the people of Cameroon. The people of Cameroon seem trapped in the post-colonial mindset as though dragged by European mandated political philosophers concerned not with issues of freedom from foreign influences, enslavement, and domination.

Chapter Two

Um Nyobe's Political Philosophy within the UPC National Liberation Struggle

Cameroonians may not seem to have come to terms with the historical challenge they faced before settling down to configure a nation. However, there is one man who proved that he had a clear understanding of the situation and knew exactly what had to be done to achieve the twin goals of national liberation and nation-building. That person is Um Nyobe. Lamentably Um Nyobe is not a well celebrated political figure in Cameroon particularly in Anglophone Cameroon. As the founder of the national liberation struggle and the nation-building project in Cameroon, Um Nyobe deserves his rightful place in history of Cameroon As the first and major step towards situating Um Nyobe in his rightful place in history, this chapter analyses his political philosophy. What about Um Nyobe's political philosophy gave the UPC the image of a national liberation movement and made Um Nyobe himself stand out as emblematic of patriotism in Cameroon? In this chapter, we will verify his political action within the national liberation movement in his mission to liberate Cameroon from European invasion and occupation. We will use Um Nyobe's political philosophy as a barometer to evaluate his political consciousness in relation to this mission. How did his political philosophy animate to transform Cameroon into a nation once he achieved the primary goal? The primary goal included the kicking out from the Cameroonian trust territories the invading European invaders exploiters and regaining freedom and total independence. According to Um Nyobe's UPC platform for a free Cameroon, independence was a three-pronged issue -- independence of thought, independence of expression and independence of action.

In analysing the political philosophy of Um Nyobe within the UPC nationalist revolution, we had to look at the foundation of his political consciousness, the programme he had outlined, and the means he used to achieve the twin goals of national liberation and forming a political system whole in form and free from imperial manipulation. In short how did he go about forming a nation? We achieved the task by relying on Um Nyobe's political writings as our main source of data. We matched these with his political activities in the struggles against the European marauders. We first examine the foundation of his political philosophy as a methodological prerequisite to understanding the source of his political consciousness and political thinking. Secondly, we explore the content of his programme to achieve the twin goals of national liberation and nation-building.

The Foundation of Um Nyobe's Revolutionary Political Philosophy

Political literature in Cameroon tends to indicate that Um Nyobe's political ideas were uncompromisingly opposed to the European mission to invade and to enslave local peoples on their own soil for the exploitation of natural resources for the growth and expansion of the European industrial economy. Um Nyobe's political ideas consisted of a socialist oriented agenda (Joseph 1978; Woungly-Massaga 1984).First, his programme evolved around two cardinal points the immediately independence of Cameroon and the reunification of its two sister territories reaped apart by European prowlers. In assessing Um Nyobe's political philosophy, we realised that the reunification of the two halves of the territory was actually part of his overall strategy aimed at uniting energies to free the occupied territories from any foreign invasion and unchecked exploitation, destruction and the dehumanisation of the people. Second, Nyobe's political philosophy consisted of building a new and united society according to the territorial limits that resulted from the German colonial practices. His revolutionary approach stemmed from the fact that he interpreted European invasion and the exploitation of the people and the material resources of Cameroon from a Marxist perspective. In that light, his socialist agenda consisted of broadening both the political realm and the economic base of Cameroon to include the various strata of society so that the people can be better able to resist any foreign occupation, the reckless exploitation of their natural wealth and the dehumanisation of their people.

An examination of the factors that might have shaped the revolutionary character of Um Nyobe's political philosophy reveals that his source of inspiration was the African indigenous world view and value system which the Bassa people share with other indigenous African societies. Using that as his philosophical foundation, he weaved other knowledge forms appropriated from other sources to obtain the desired effect. His African indigenous world view and value system played a crucial role in fashioning his resolve in the fight for freedom; fight against social injustice and criminal practices perpetrated on local people. Konde (1998) maintains that the Bassa knowledge and value system institutionalised in the *Nge* governance institution that grooms the *mbombok*, the Bassa leaders, gave Um Nyobe the resolute determination against social injustice and particularly against foreign invasion and domination. Mbembe (1984) also acknowledges this fact. Konde (ibid) advances a theory that Um Nyobe's revolutionary political consciousness was rooted in the value system of the African people, epitomised by the Bassa concept of human freedom based on the autonomy of the individual. According to Konde, the value system of the African people epitomised by the Bassa concept of human freedom is revolutionarily opposed to any form of foreign invasion of other people's societies. The abusive practices and the destructive systems of thought that were introduced by the European marauders were most likely to restrict human freedom and curtail the autonomy of the individual were forms of social injustice vehemently denounced and resisted.

As someone who was yet unspoiled by the alienating effects of Western education and bourgeois ideas (Konde 1998: 47), he stood for no other thing than human freedom Um Nyobe, had risen within the Bassa social system up to the rank of *Mpodol,* a position that is held by lineage heads, Mpodol functioned as models of civic leadership in Bassa society. Um Nyobe eventually was named *Mpodol lon* by the Bassa people and given the mandate to lead the struggle for freedom from the invasion, occupation, enslavement, and the destruction of Cameroon by the European invaders and armed robbers. Under his astute leadership, the diasporic faction of the Bamileke in the Mungo area used proceeds of economic activities to resist the French. The Bamileke people thus joined the Bassa people in the struggle and gave it a push gradually embracing all Cameroonians into the struggle.

Groomed in a value system that opposes injustice, only two things existed: something is either right or it is wrong and wisdom, demands that that which is wrong be rejected outright, without compromise. The invasion of other people's society is wrong since this hampers human freedom and so should be rejected. Um Nyobe's long involvement in the activities of the labour syndicates, training as a magistrate's clerk, and his affinity and association with groups sharing a Marxist world-view enabled Um Nyobe oppose the designs and mission of invading and destructive Europeans, but to understand and it to appropriate its internal logic for use against them. Um Nyobe's training in education with the protestant mission provided him the impetus with which to effectively appropriate the internal logic of the European invaders. Indeed he his revolutionary thinking sprung from these sources in his struggle against European invasion and enslavement of local people.

Um Nyobe effectively situated his arguments within the legal and institutional framework put in place by the European invaders themselves. Thus he argued deftly against the adoption of a policy of assimilation by the French invaders. According to Um Nyobe, the policy of assimilation the French attempted ran contrary to the republican institutions in France. He argued that the policy denied Cameroonians in their own county the same rights of citizenship the French citizens enjoyed in France should be rejected outright with no compromise. Additionally his main arguments focused on the reckless exploitation of Cameroon's resources and the dehumanisation of local peoples by the European invaders. He focussed particularly these arguments as they pertained to the Bassa region, his home area, noting that it served as a labour reserve neighbourhood successively during the period of the German invasion as well as during that of the French invaders (Konde 1998). His Marxist orientation woven into his Bassa home-grown knowledge and value system, broadened his approach in his campaigns against social injustice and his resolute struggle for freedom. The French, indeed, the Europeans desperate to invade and dispossess, found Um Nyobe's argumentation unpalatable. His political idea aimed at uniting all Cameroonians against the invasion of the land by Europeans predators who had the intention of enslaving Cameroonians to work to produce for the European budding industrial economy.

This could explain why the accession of Um Nyobe to the leadership of the UPC subsequent to its inception in 1948, radicalised politics in the then European occupied territory of Cameroon. This rise gave Cameroonians the hope and the courage to challenge the European invasion of Cameroon, especially in light of France's intentions to exploit the free labour of Cameroonians. This criminal scheme was in line with the ambition of the French to raise France to the status of a powerful nation, or to achieve the dream of a greater France by integrating the conquered and subjugated overseas territories into the French Republic (Joseph 1978). Um Nyobe's ability to radicalise politics was made possible because he had built a political idea that revolutionarily countered all of the European devices and designs and was resolute in his pursuits to rally Cameroonians into one main stream of consciousness. Um Nyobe's stand to kick both the French and the British out of

Cameroon and to regain freedom from the Europeans was articulated by the UPC national liberation movement. Um Nyobe was not yet in the category of estranged Cameroonians alienated from their physical world and rendered powerless. His feet were still firmly rooted in the Bassa soil. Western education and the religious type of missionary Christianity, while instrumental, had had a minimal effect on his political consciousness.

His was deeply-rooted the Bassa indigenous cosmology. And this deep-rootedness enabled him to be resolute in his political action plan. Yet Um Nyobe attempted to understand the designs and intentions of the marauding European forces from a socialist approach to politics. Nevertheless, he never openly identified with communism. He was persuaded to the core that by openly identifying with communism he would imbibe a foreign value system. To him, imbibing a foreign value system would have been counterproductive in the struggle and would have facilitated the European invasion, dehumanisation and destruction. Firstly anti-Europeanism entailed belonging to none of the ideological camps of the European aggressors. Secondly, it was dangerous to back any invading country against another because, though they may seem to be ideologically divided, a certain level of solidarity exists between them. Thus he rejected all accusations that the UPC was a communist party. His rebuttals of UPC communist party affiliation was demonstrated in his declaration during the first UPC Congress held in Dschang on April 10, 1950:

> "They treat us as communists, but everybody knows that we are not a communist organisation. We are not saying so because we cannot become communists, but because we consider that the fight for our national liberation does not take into account this or that ideology. This struggle is

incumbent on all Africans of good will whatever their opinion, their religious conviction, or social position."[10]

Political party in the classical sense was not the best option in the anti-European invasion struggle as well. Cameroonians needed a platform through which thoughts can develop and actions canalised to struggle for freedom. Hence, the political panacea for the fight for national liberation was a movement comprised of men and women of all social categories, revolutionary in character, with the orientation to unite efforts to throw out the foreign forces of occupation and destruction. This viewpoint was backed by his argument against the view that Cameroon was a poor country advanced by the French invaders as justification for their mission of invasion. Even if Cameroon was a poor country, he maintained, that was no justification for invasion and domination. He wondered why on earth European marauding forces would invade and occupy a poor country. Because robbers don't rob poor people it was needless to be in two minds between ideological camps or to be soft or negotiating with thieves who have come to kill and destroy ones wealth to enrich themselves while claiming that they are doing so because one is poor.

With this absurdity in mind and as a Pan-Cameroonist, and Pan-Africanist, he situated his political idea within a broader socio-temporal context. The fight for freedom and emancipation from European imperial domination, manipulation, and destruction could be achieved only by the exploited people of the *third world* bonding themselves together and rising up together The UPC may have been conceived with such ideals in mind because upon its creation on April 10th 1948, the party set out straightaway to unite the inhabitants of the territory. The first article of the UPC statutes tends to confirm this point. Article one of the UPC statutes was in fact resolute

---

[10] Translation is mine.

about the drive to regain the lost humanity of colonised subjects from European forces through the collective efforts of all Cameroonians.

Furthermore, the global political reforms following the end of World War II and the creation the powerful and imposing imperialist United Nations, created a window of hope in Um Nyobe for his liberation struggle. Reform stimulated him and determined the role he was to play in his stewardship of the UPC liberation struggle in Cameroon. He saw reform as an opportunity to raise objections within its framework to foreign domination. Through domination the Cameroonian People had been dragged into a deadly war in Europe at no fault of theirs. Unfortunately, this stimulation and hope became a source of disillusionment for Um Nyobe. The promise of peace reverberating hope throughout the colonised world upon the creation of the United Nations actually did raise the level of Um Nyobe's political consciousness and determined the political actions of the UPC liberation movement. Tragically, for Um Nyobe hope for peace instead finally ended in his brutal murder in 1958.

Through news publications, such as *La Voix du Cameroun*, a UPC journal, he had raised the voices of the exploited people onto the international scene. Even Douala Manga Bell, as an elected representative of Cameroon to the UN, failed to provide such a voice. With scant knowledge of the legal profession, Um Nyobe could see that the trusteeship status of French Cameroon created an arbitrary situation. He came up with a political idea to use the very legal instruments of the European invaders within the framework provided by the newly created international governing body, the UN, to address this arbitrariness. France wanted to surreptitiously integrate Cameroon into the French empire under an arbitrary law. Unfortunately, the UN did not prove helpful to him in this struggle. Official representatives from Cameroon to the UN were fraudulently selected by France through an electoral process that Um Nyobe described as politically fraudulent (*escroqueries politiques*). Douala Manga Bell etc., including a Frenchman, Dr. Aujoulat, were giving a wrong picture of the real situation on the ground in Cameroon to the international community thus obscuring it. This fraudulent representation prevented him from gaining access to the international podium where he could present the true picture of what was obtaining on the ground in Cameroon.

In spite of the fact that both the UN and France seem to have been playing for time, each of them in their own sphere, while the dehumanisation of the people of Cameroon and the destruction of the cultural and natural resources of the land went on, the revolutionary posture of Um Nyobe within the UPC liberation movement was not deterred. In the final analysis, the French thieves, killers and destroyers, together with their European cousins, including the UN structure with local support all combined their tactics and made the national liberation struggle for the UPC an impossible one to achieve. In spite of Um Nyobe's determination and revolutionary approach in the struggle to throw out the European thieves determined to stay and in place a system for the defence of their continuous exploitation. Unfortunately for Um Nyobe, the European thieves had put in place every possible strategy to frustrate the UPC liberation movement. Joseph (1974) observes that the Um Nyobe led liberation movement was fast gaining grounds all over the national territory as a mass movement but was faced with insurmountable barricades on its way to freedom. Legally, a barricade of laws were promulgated by the government in Paris, voted by the French parliament, supported by the infamous article 76 of the UN charter, upheld and implemented by their local valets in Cameroon.

Structurally, Um Nyobe found himself battling within an overbearing institutional framework (Zang-Atangana 1989). To make matters worse, France recruited mercenaries of misinformation and misrepresentation to give a wrong picture of the situation in Cameroon. Some of these mercenaries were unfortunately Cameroonians. The mercenaries found expression in political parties. The creation of political parties and ethnic associations under the pretext of multi-party politics, instigated and sponsored by France, bore a hidden intention -- to fragment political opinion, divert attention away from the genuine liberation movement, and then sabotage it. Some of these political parties were either sponsored by the French or were created by French nationals in Cameroon. The Frenchman, Dr. Louis Paul Aujoulat actually formed a political party in Cameroon to create confusion on the political scene

Both the legal and institutional frameworks put in place by the European invaders, sapped Um Nyobe's energy, played for time and diverted attention away from the substance of the matter, which was that the Europeans should simply pack their bags and leave. The military presence played the repressive aspect of it. In spite of the diverse trials and temptations, however, Um Nyobe kept his political thought on target. During the first UPC congress in Dschang on April 10, 1950, he cautioned his militants not to be dissuaded from active involvement in politics:

> "... If we do not engage ourselves in politics, which consist of fighting by all means, and in all forms, for the emancipation of our country, we leave the field free for the colonialists to carry out their political criminality, to practice force labour, *indegénat*, shameless exploitation of our riches and the imprisonment and assassination of our people.
>
> Today all people of goodwill have understood that freedom is gained only by fighting for it, and there we are not alone. Throughout the whole world the forces of democracy are fighting victoriously against the forces of oppression and imperialism..."[11]

However, his failure to seek redress to the question of inhumanity by man towards man through legal means and through official channels did not deter him. He kept the fire

---

[11] Translation is mine.

within him burning brightly that the cause for freedom was moral and just. His indefatigability further strengthened the revolutionary posture of the UPC. He signed two very important declarations of the UPC in 1954. In the declarations, the UPC made a clarion call for the restoration of the land of Cameroon with immediate accession to statehood and independence. The French used it to declare war on the people of Cameroon by banning the UPC in 1955. The French ended up brutally murdering Um Nyobe, it's Secretary General and nationalist leader, in 1958 under the infamous *loi-cadre* that instituted the French military occupation of Cameroon. The UN, did nothing about a situation that held back peace in spite of the fact that the 11th session of the UN General Assembly had demanded that France restore normal political life in Cameroon. France consequently militarily occupied the Cameroonian territory and got away with it, brutally killing Um Nyobe in the process.

After Um Nyobe's death, however, a more ground-breaking faction of the UPC emerged. Having resolutely established the revolutionary character of the UPC, the adherents of this ground-breaking faction went underground and fought in the *maquis* to the last drop of their blood in 1971. Regrettably, the French eventually annihilated this ground-breaking faction of the UPC with local support, with the aid of Ahmadou Ahidjo who had volunteered to be the local representative of the European gang of thieves. After killing and steeling, the Europeans were poised for the total destruction of Cameroon. Illegality prevailed under the regime of President Ahmadou Ahidjo who opted to support the French with a local gang of thieves thus allowing the French to effectively play an invisible but decisive back-stage role. These developments, though negative, confirmed Um Nyobe's conception that "all Americo-European ideological camps and institutions belonged to a coalition of a capitalist order, intended only to exploit and to enslave the other races of the world". On this perception about Europeans the revolutionary nature of his political idea took root. On the other hand Um Nyobe had always warned against blind nationalism. By blind nationalism, Um Nyobe meant a nationalism that may be trapped in a compromise with the invaders advertently or inadvertently (see Um Nyobe 1957; 1961).

Um Nyobe's Political Programme

Um Nyobe's political programme was derived directly from his political philosophy, which anathemises social injustice particularly the invasion and occupation of Cameroon by Europeans. This political philosophy was intended to be ploughed back to nurture its foundation, meaning that he had intended to birth a nation in Cameroon that was truly autonomous, not an appendage of another nation or group of nations. In an address dated December 15, 1951 delivered at the UPC Pan-Cameroon Congress, Um Nyobe once more articulated the basis of his anti-European occupation of Cameroon in which he cautioned against the civilisation theory. Cautioning against the civilisation theory which he said was a smokescreen to enslave Africans on their own soil:

> "We are told that the whites came to Africa to civilise the "savages", and unfortunately, some of our compatriots have been tempted to believe in such a theory. Those who consider such theories ignore the fact that the colonialist came to the African coast with no other agenda than to search for resources that would foster the expansion of the European market economy. In their adventures in the coast of Africa they introduced slave trade through which they massively exported blacks from Africa to slave in the plantations in Central America belonging to the European colonialists. And when they claimed to have abolished slave trade in 1848 it was transformed into FORCED LABOUR

on our land, which they declared vacant, without an owner, and appropriated it as their property to exploit"[12].

He stated unequivocally that it would be inadmissible to contemplate any political solution to the Cameroon problem without taking into account the fact that its daunting problems were brought into being by the invasion and occupation of its territory by European thieves, killers and destroyers. This would be like a doctor trying to administer treatment to a patient without having made the proper diagnosis. Um Nyobe's political consciousness arose from his inbuilt abhorrence of the European invasion and occupation of Cameroon. His programme for Cameroon directly responded to this aggression. He firmly rooted his programme in the indigenous African value system that eschews foreign dictatorship and domination. (Serequeberhan 2002). The UPC was born as part of the post-war movements to galvanise efforts towards ending colonial rule in the colonised world. Um Nyobe sought no compromise with Europeans. In his stewardship of the UPC, Um Nyobe was also fully conscious politically of the fragmentation that had occurred within the Cameroonian social and political environment and the consequences this had engendered on the emerging political structure or social system.

He was aware, for example, the missionaries' type of religious Christianity was making inroad into the land and that churches based on this type of Christianity were proliferating. This religious hegemony coupled with the creation of ethnic based associations and political parties, orchestrated by the Europeans contributed to the fragmentation of the social and political environment of Cameroonian society. He was also aware that the two major divisions of Cameroon along two European colonial linguistic lines of French and English further compounded this situation. Hence, unity of the people was

---

[12] Translation is mine.

paramount in the national liberation struggle. He was fully aware that the European forces of invasion and occupation intentionally introduced these devices and ideological instruments to create such fragmentation in order to frustrate the emergence of a united liberation front so as to maintain dominion over colonised subjects.

To address this situation, Um Nyobe's political programme, which was to build a country that is totally united included the immediate reunification of the two halves of the Cameroon territory that had been ripped apart by France and Great Britain. For an effective political action against this menace Um Nyobe proposed a forum to unite all political forces in the occupied territory towards creating a common Cameroonian consciousness. He proposed the creation of a "Kamerun United National Committee" to galvanise all political action to attain immediate reunification and then achieve independence, a stated time limit for the end of the trusteeship status of Cameroon, and the revision of the trusteeship accord to reflect the wishes of the population. He called for the suppression of the proviso that intends to integrate Cameroon into the French empire, adding that Cameroonians should also guard against any attempt by the British to integrate any part of Cameroon into Nigeria. This call seemed to have been heeded to and the Kamerun United National Congress (KUNC) was created in the British occupied territory of Cameroon with Dibongue Jabea and Dr. Endeley as its president and vice president respectively. And on Friday August 22, 1952, at Tiko the UPC led by Um Nyobe and Abel Kingue met with the KUNC where they made a joint declaration on the immediate reunification of Cameroon and called on the colonial administrations to make concrete proposals about Cameroon's attainment of independence.

At its Second Congress at Eseka, which held from the 28th to the 30th September 1952, the UPC officially adopted reunification as part of its political programme. The UPC also adopted its political action plan for a reunified Cameroon as follows:

- The institution of a single Administration in Cameroon;
- The creation of one Legislative Assembly;
- The establishment of a Governing Council with elected representatives drawn from all over the country, 4/5 of which were to be Cameroonians;
- The abolition of the Trusteeship Agreement, which placed the status of Cameroon at an ambiguous situation;
- The fixing of a period for Cameroon's accession to independence as an autonomous state.

To test the pulse of Cameroonians on the reunification issue, Um Nyobe conducted a mini referendum on it in 1953 at another UPC congress that held again at Kumba from April 28 to 30, 1953, wherein out of 90 voters 83 voted for and 7 voted against. It should be noted that Um Nyobe's reunification agenda had a double objective. Firstly, to convince the UN that Cameroonians were in one agreement on the problem of the trusteeship rule, and secondly, to unite living forces in Cameroon against foreign occupation and domination. This double-faceted political agenda was in line with his political programme, which was to bequeath to Cameroonians a country totally free from foreign occupation, purely democratic, in peace, and united by a religious belief (sic), and a parliamentary system of government. Europeans chose not to listen to the voice of reason, and after eliciting the support of other political parties across the national territory, in 1954, Um Nyobe's UPC took a more revolutionary turn in favour of immediate independence.

He did not propose a language that was to replace the two European colonial languages of French and English as a uniting factor. Also, he did not abandon the religious belief he talked about. His political agenda was to establish a reunified, united and strong political entity. With respect to the question of tribalism his political response was to fight against it, not by detribalising, but rather by ensuring that ethnicity should constitute the matrix for the development of a national culture.

In that respect, he also envisaged respect for ethnic minority rights as the country was to engage in a dialectical process for the formation of a natural culture.

Politically, he was to build a society where there was freedom of association, freedom of opinion, and freedom of expression, and which was politically equal in status to France or great Britain, etc., with no iota of subservience by Cameroon to any other country. This explains his insistence that Cameroon should gain both reunification and independence immediately in order to enter into relations with other countries as an independent, united, and sovereign country. To him, any agreement that was approved by the parliament of another country was not binding on Cameroon. Above all, he was going to prove that a country's accession to political independent did not call for a situation of financial or economic begging that result in dependence. (See Joseph 1986:218 for an elaborate picture of Um Nyobe's political programme).

In terms of the structural hierarchy or political organisation within the national territory, Um Nyobe's Cameroon was to be what the UPC had referred to as a "democratic centralism". This type of a centralised democracy was to be both centripetal and centrifugal and correspond to the hierarchical structure and organisation of the UPC party itself, and would follow the natural political units of society. Communities or any other significant strata within the political base of society were to constitute political units organised as stipulated by article 6 of the UPC statute. Regional political units would follow these building blocks. The central government organs, would retain constitutional guardianship over the local and regional political units.

This model of "democratic centralism", would operate on two basic principles 1) the wishes of the population at the base of the political pyramid would transmit to the pinnacle of power as accurately as possible in a centripetal manner for formulation into policy and 2) the decisions taken at the pinnacle of power or at the centre would transmit from the centre to the political power base and applied in a centrifugal manner through channels of communication that kept both the centre and the power base permanently in touch. This means that all policy prescriptions from the centre of power were based on the wishes of the people would elect all the representatives with minimum intervention from the centre. The elected deputies or representatives not to passively bear messages to the centre or blindly impose the decisions of the centre on the people. They were to engage actively and involve themselves in the daily affairs of the people so that decisions from the centre would reflect reality. (See Zang-Atangana 1989:124).

Um Nyobe's Economic Programme

At the Second UPC Congress at Eseka Um Nyobe hinted at the nature of the UPC economic programme. Um Nyobe hinted that the UPC government would suppress custom's barriers between the two territories and centralise the budget for the development of infrastructure and for industrialisation. Industrialisation would transform local economies. The economic organisation of Cameroon would be broad-based. Um Nyobe envisaged a system of economic production wherein every region would organise itself into economic units create economic structures and systems of production and distribution controlled and managed by the people themselves. Such an economic structure was consistent with Um Nyobe's political idea to encourage teamwork toward long term benefits through well-organised corporative associations and other forms of economic structures. These structures were to be independent of political parties.

Um Nyobe, never spared any opportunity to emphasise Cameroon's rich natural endowments. He sought to organise society in such a way that people had access to these resources so they could exploit it for their own benefits. Accordingly, he encouraged a spirit of syndicalism throughout the entire national territory. Worker's rights and social well-being were to be constantly ensured. At the state level, Um Nyobe's UPC government would nationalise the corporations and banks in order to create and manage a national currency detached from any foreign currency. Um Nyobe's UPC government would also preserve and nourish a private economic sector for both national and foreign investment with conditions of mutual agreement between these two sectors, and also between them and the state within a system of a democratically planned economy, but with the general orientation towards achieving economic independence for the country. Legislation would minimise foreign economic influences. The UPC government would discourage commoditisation of land, and put in place a structure to study and document the rich natural resources of Cameroon including those under the soils and under the seas.

In the domain of industry, Um Nyobe's UPC government would emphasize import substitution by investing in giant industrial sectors and mechanisation of agriculture. These approaches were wrapped in an ideological framework that viewed negatively international agreement economic effect on developing countries. This was the basis of his emphasis on local transformation.

Um Nyobe's Social Programme

Um Nyobe envisioned a society with equal treatment of all persons regardless of race or ethnicity. Um Nyobe's UPC government, if he ever had the opportunity to come to power, would enact a new labour law to counter the colonial labour legislation of 1946 and meet the aspirations of all Cameroonians. This would ensure that all Cameroonians enjoyed the benefits of their labour. There would be no taxation on income earnings. There would be no taxation without the provision of social amenities. He also envisioned the reversal of the land legislation introduced by the British in which all the land in its occupied territory became Crown land.

Such a government would invest heavily in the health sector, and put in place health policy that ensured free access to health care. This investment in health would include medical research, the development of health infrastructure and the development of medical personnel at all levels. It was to lay emphasis on education at all levels within a lay system of education controlled solely by the state. The 1952 Eseka plan of action through the centralisation of the state budget would enable the development of educational infrastructure to minimise the rate at which Cameroonians were going to study abroad.

Um Nyobe's Cultural Programme

Um Nyobe based his cultural programme on Western education. He planned to broaden it to include all segments of society. Um Nyobe's UPC government would put in place a free education policy to ensure mass education for all who needed it. He recognised that the ethnic cultures of the peoples of Cameroon were a source of cultural wealth for an independent, reunified, and united Cameroon. Hence, he tailored his cultural programme in such a way that the various cultural traditions were to interact in a dialectical process that would gradually lead to the establishment of a national culture.

Um Nyobe's Strategy

Um Nyobe's strategy - the line of attack to deploy his vision – was organisation and mobilisation. The strength of the UPC national liberation movement was organisation and mobilisation (Joseph 1974: 442; Zang-Atangana 1989:123). The organisational and rallying abilities of Um Nyobe also maintained the discipline and the solidarity within the ranks of the movement and made it a political force with which to reckon. The UPC political slogan that "no proper organisation, no possible victory," bore testimony of Um Nyobe's organisational and rallying abilities. This was directly reflected in the discipline and the solidarity within the ranks of the movement. In terms of the financial means to run his government, he intended to encourage the mobilisation of social forces for the accumulation of indigenous capital through a process in which the citizens were fully responsible for their destiny and have total control of their God-given natural resources, while the government was to be in charge of foreign trade.

The organisational dimension of Um Nyobe's political idea for nation-building in Cameroon was thus going to constitute his main strategy through which the desired goal and mission was going to be achieved His political idea of democratic centralism, which could also be seen as being at the base of his reunification and one Cameroon drive, aimed not only at building a united political entity but at moulding a common Cameroonian consciousness, skills, values, beliefs, and a common behavioural pattern through the process of socialisation. He identified religion as a structural prerequisite that can provide a sense of common purpose and existence to members of a society towards achieving an economic objective. He harboured hostility towards the religious Christianity of the missionaries and the views of some of its clergy because these tended to undermine the national liberation struggle.

His attempt at uniting thoughts and actions throughout the national territory towards a common goal was the basis for the development of a national identity and national consciousness. Yet he preserved the ethnic basis of identity. In the domains of politics and the economy, his political philosophy consisted of laying down the conditions that would produce certain cultural patterns that encouraged teamwork, patience, and hard work among the citizens including the creation of corporative associations based on the principles of "self-reliant and auto-transformation." The name of the movement itself, the union of the populations of Cameroon, and the way it was structured could be seen as an embodiment of a political idea that builds on self-organisation as a strategy for rallying efforts and energies for social, economic, and political achievements against foreign domination.

Although Um Nyobe never had the opportunity to implement his political idea for the liberation of Cameroon and the establishment of a nation in Cameroon, before his cruel death in the hands of French military arsenal in collusion with their local allies, he had made his point clear and stood for it throughout the UPC struggle for freedom, namely; that the European presence in Cameroon was illegal and thus unwanted.

Having come up with the idea to create the UPC, the statutes were pre-planned and written in Paris by Gaston Donnat. This was because, as the above theory advanced by Kegne Pokam goes, the French had intended to use the UPC only as a window dressing to manage the power of the growing proletariats and to justify the dual presence of both capitalism and socialism, all Western ideologies, and also to use that to demonstrate how capitalism was crushing socialism. The UPC was besides the workers syndicate and the civil service, all created by the French. Unfortunately, Um Nyobe, who stood for justice against evil, surprised the French by refusing to toe the line of the French Socialist Party as did Senghor and Houphouet-Boigny. For having run away with a French idea, the French had to kill Um Nyobe and then destroy the UPC.

The killing of Um Nyobe and the subsequent killing of other UPC leaders and the complete wiping out of the UPC national liberation movement can also be understood from the perspective that it was coming at a very crucial moment in European history wherein they were just emerging from the war that had completely devastated Europe which then badly needed reconstruction. The French had just discovered oil deposits in the Wouri Delta in 1947. This was one of the major mineral resources that were crucial in her post-war reconstruction project inaugurated in 1954. This time coincided with the peak of the UPC uprising against the European invasion, occupation of Cameroon and the stealing of its resources. It is in this light that we can see the role of Ahmadou Ahidjo as a local ally and collaborator in to enslave black people to destroy their societies and to cart off the booty to Europe for the economic benefit of Europe rather than as a nationalist.

Chapter Three

Ahmadou Ahidjo's Political Ideas for Nation-Building

Following the murder of Um Nyobe by French soldiers who had also completely annihilated the UPC national liberation movement, the stage was set for the philosophers who were mandated by Europeans to think the nation in Cameroon to triumph. Ahmadou Ahidjo who became the first president of the Republic of Cameroon and who was the first of the philosophers who were mandated by Europeans to think the nation in Cameroon, is the focus of this chapter. This chapter examines what Ahmadou Ahidjo had put up as a political philosophy for his nation- building endeavour in Camero0n. Before we delve into making an analysis of Ahmadou Ahidjo's political philosophy, we should properly compare and contrast Um Nyobe with Ahmadou Ahidjo. Um Nyobe who, as the initiator of the national liberation project, not only in Cameroon but also in the whole of French occupied Black Africa, who emerged from the ranks of an indigenous society formulated a home-grown political philosophy intended to gradually crystallise into a protective ideology against the European invasion of Cameroon. President Ahmadou Ahidjo on the contrary was made by the European invading powers. Consequently, the happening of Ahmadou Ahidjo on the political scene was part of the counter-revolutionary strategy by France against the fight for national freedom and national independence in Cameroon. Although Ahmadou Ahidjo had militated in the floating political party, the *Bloc Democratic Camerounais* (BDC) of Dr. Aujoulat, a French man whom he had always sided with, becoming a councillor in the French Parliament, he is known to have all along been a silent listener in the French parliament (Joseph 1978: 45). Until January 18,

1958 when he made his first public speech at the occasion of his investiture as Cameroon's second Prime Minister, Ahmadou Ahidjo is not on record as having made any public statement with a nationalist intent or of any kind in relation to the national liberation, nation-building project in Cameroon.

In examining the political philosophy of Ahmadou Ahidjo, we are in fact examining the political philosophy of someone who was appointed by a French government official in Cameroon to become the second Prime Minister of East Cameroon and who later on became the President of the Republic. We are thus examining what a French appointee had outlined as a political philosophy in that capacity with programmes and strategies that were to enable him to attain the goal of national liberation and nation-building in Cameroon. We are hereby examining what Ahmadou Ahidjo later on said he was going to do with Cameroon in the political, economic, social and cultural domains as contained in his speeches and other political writings of his. An alternative inquiry would seek to find out if Ahmadou Ahidjo had, by chance, come up with an original idea about what he wanted to do in relation to the challenge at hand or was he a victim of the prevailing post-colonial thought that characterised post-colonial Africa, wrapped up in the self-important notion of development that hoodwinked post-war African countries into the logic of Europe's target to enslave non-European societies?

The Origins of Ahidjoism in Cameroon

In the particular case of Cameroon, Ahidjoism by definition is a mode of thinking that does not belief the self as its own subject but rather believes the self as an object of the subjecting subject. The following paragraphs will shed light on how this this mode of thinking affected Cameroon and Cameroonians. President Ahmadou Ahidjo's political ideas for Cameroon might have been broad-based, judging from his political writings, but as a pragmatist or practical person if you like, he based his political actions purely on the political-economic domain as propagated by the European Mute on the national liberation issue, he focused only on the nation-building project which he attempted to root on a foreign foundation philosophy. A proper understanding of the foundation of Ahmadou Ahidjo's political philosophy can be understood only by going beyond the political philosophy itself to understand the foreign political forces that fashioned his world view, which did not give him an opportunity to root his political ideas on a home-grown political philosophy in a way that will enable the nation to be growing at the same time as it is nourishing the home-grown foundation philosophy of its birth. Ahmadou Ahidjo, like Um Nyobe, may not have been highly educated from the point of view of his attainment within the system of western education, but unlike Um Nyobe, whose political ideas developed from and indigenous source, Ahmadou Ahidjo did not develop a home-grown political philosophy.

As a graduate from the Yaoundé Higher Elementary School (primary school) from where he later on trained as a postal clerk, and, unlike Um Nyobe who was well educated within his Bassa indigenous world view and value system, still rooted in the Bassa soil, as a Muslim, Ahmadou Ahidjo's early contact with the European invading forces of occupation trimmed him bare of any Muslim radicalism against imperial domination. Having been trimmed bare of any Muslim radicalism against imperial domination, he was rather transformed into a participant. He could not finish his Islamic education in Garoua but was transferred to a secular primary school and was later on politically groomed within the ranks of the French politicians, which tainted his political ideas and made him see the French criminality in Cameroon from the point of view of the criminals. He saw the Europeans as partners in the nation-building project. As an estranged person who grew up having no political judgment of his own, having been psychologically damaged with bourgeoisified modes of perception, it was very easy for the French to subject Ahmadou Ahidjo to the status of a valet or string-puppet, which they used against Cameroonians instead of the other way round.

From the look of things, Ahmadou Ahidjo seems to have been an unprincipled person whom the French had very easily brought under control and manipulation. He neither belonged to the camp of the soft nationalists in which was to be found J.N. Foncha and Dr. E.M.L. Endeley, nor to the camp of the moderate constitutional nationalists in which was to be found Soppo Priso, not to talk of belonging to the camp of the revolutionary nationalist in which was to be found Um Nyobe, Dr. Felix Moumié, Abel Kingue, Ernest Ouandié, etc. As an unprincipled person, he was at best an agent of foreign capital. Historical accounts have it that immediately Um Nyobe was killed, Ahmadou Ahidjo took off for France. He flew to France where he negotiated with General Charles de Gaulle for France to re-entrust or sublet the UN trusteeship territories to him so that he could henceforth assume the role of managing its affairs on behalf of France. He is supposed to have promised to General Charles de Gaulle to work hard to integrate the British invaded territory into the French political arrangement. He succeeded and thus became the new face of France in Cameroon. To give himself a veneer of legitimacy, Ahmadou Ahidjo indistinctly espoused the key aspects of the UPC programme while France took the back stage and was still controlling the Assembly, providing the necessary logistical support, imposing a military and other agreements and directives (Joseph 1978). Rooted in no principles of his, Ahmadou Ahidjo could only develop a political philosophy that was thus collaborative of European invasion and destruction.

Unlike Um Nyobe who was groomed within the *Nge* academy of social stratification and governance of the Bassa land according to from where he gained his political ideas, and who was thus mandated by the indigenous Bassa people to lead the liberation struggle for Cameroon, an act which legitimised his political engagements in the struggle for freedom in Cameroon according to Konde (1989:49), Ahmadou Ahidjo was introduced into politics by foreigners who also groomed him. In this case, the foreigners who groomed Ahmadou Ahidjo were the French. His close association with Louis-Paul Aujoulat right from the early days of his political career provided him the opportunity for the French to groom him. As Ahmadou Ahidjo was thus a French impostor whose political ideas were not home-grown. Bayart (1980: 160) indicates that because Ahmadou Ahidjo was a French impostor, certain Lamidos who were instead perturbed about him did not give him their benediction because they instead considered Ahmadou Ahidjo to be a "Young Turk." In the case of Ahmadou Ahidjo,

> "It should not be overlooked that it was a Frenchman, Rocaglia (Representative in the Cameroon Assembly), who encouraged the future President of the Republic to enter politics, and that a section of the French administration supported his candidature in 1956. Moreover, Ahidjo had participated – though as a Muslim, marginally – in the very moderate *Bloc Démocratique Camerounais* of Dr. Aujoulat [a Frenchman] since 1952" (Bayart in Joseph 1978: 45).

Then again, in 1947, when he was a postal clerk in Garoua, the French man Guy Georgy actually fished out Ahmadou Ahidjo and encouraged him to go into politics. Mandated by the French, which the people of Cameroon were fighting to free themselves from their stranglehold, a fight that was articulated by the UPC, it is easy to see that Ahmadou Ahidjo neither had a political idea that was founded in any home-grown world view, nor did he speak on behalf of any indigenous voice, but had a mission as mandated by the French to represent their political-economic interest in Cameroon. Mandated by the French to represent their political-economic interest in Cameroon Ahmadou Ahidjo could not have been ground-breaking. All what he became familiar with was the prevailing post-colonial discourse of the time. The French predators, for their part, whose designs and mission in Cameroon were never intended for the benefit of the Cameroonian people, but to steal, loot, rob, and enslave the people, preferred Ahmadou Ahidjo to Soppo Priso, even though the latter had been president of the Assembly. The former had proved that he could be used as an astute manager of a French over sea's concern by his loyalty to his masters from Paris. He was to later on prove his ability to implement programmes that were designed in Paris as accurately as possible. Unfortunately, programmes that were designed in Paris were actually intended to lure, blind fool and to douse the flame of national liberation in Cameroonians with disastrous consequences on the people of Cameroon.

It becomes obvious at this point that Ahmadou Ahidjo's political philosophy was based on a transitory illusion, not deeply rooted in the social, cultural, political and economic realities of Cameroon. As a French impostor he came to define his mission in Cameroon to be that of assisting the European in their mission to Africa which was to steal, kill and destroy. He was thus a francesised Cameroonian Muslim who represented foreign interests in Cameroon, and served as president of Cameroon in that capacity from 1958 to 1982 when he left office. His strategy consisted mainly of using brute force coupled with the law and enticements to produce the new man in Cameroon who should be yielding to European mission to Africa which was to steal, kill and destroy.

Unlike Um Nyobe who had a ground-breaking political idea and an agenda of his own, and whose anti-European invasion stance enabled him to address himself to issues specifically, analytically and in depth, President Ahmadou Ahidjo was a tongue-wagging politician whose secret agenda to impose the political and economic will of the European invaders on Cameroonians could not be hidden permanently. His lose style of writing in which he merely touched on issues and without the intention to engage people's innermost thoughts and imagination as to commit them to action easily brings to the fore an inward state of a vague and subjective mind. With no intention to engage people's innermost thoughts and imagination as to commit them to action, also points to a man who had no clear political philosophy of his own and no real commitment to the pursuit of an objective towards achieving the goal of national liberation and nation-building. The psychology of repression may not be imminent in Ahmadou Ahidjo's political writings though, but his political practices contrast sharply with his political philosophy. As a military ruler in Muslim attire, and as a man who subverted the national liberation struggle, it is possible that he may have intended to reconcile himself with history by drawing attention away from his acts of terrorism on Cameroonians with documentary evidence that portray him as a political thinker and great statesman.

In any case, it is clear from the events that led up to his enthronement at the helm of the Cameroon nation by France that Ahmadou Ahidjo was not in the camp of the national liberators who stood against the exploitation and the destruction of Cameroon by the European invaders and forces of occupation. He was a collaborator, his long and close collaboration with the French in Cameroon, and his willingness to collaborate in the killing of Um Nyobe and in the destruction of the UPC national liberation movement, attest to this. Coming from a Muslim background, and considering the Ahmed Ben Bella factor in Algeria, he was purposefully groomed politically as a collaborator and so could not have been opposed to his metropolitan mentors in any way. His political philosophy could only have been fashioned by the perception that confirmed his collaborative stance, rooted on an agenda to establish close ties with the European invaders at all cost. In the 4th Congress of the UC (*Union Camerounaise*) Party on July 4–8, 1962 at Ebolowa, he announced that collaboration with the European invaders had benefits. He said:

> "At present, Cameroon economy bears the stigmas of colonialism. But the achievements of colonialism have not always been negative. We have in fact an infrastructure, an

economic ground-work, which we intend to exploit skilfully (agriculture, staff, economic and administrative organisation, roads, railways, telecommunications, ports, etc.). Cameroon derives benefits from the existence of important private concerns. The work to be undertaken is that of reconversion, of adaptation, and not of a systematic destruction".

From the other side of the cheek, in the same speech cited above, he could also observe that:

"Cameroon, having scarcely recovered from the convalescence of the colonial dependence, is still under foreign domination, to such an extent that her trade balance to say the least boarders upon deficit".

Today, over half a century after Ahmadou Ahidjo made this observation, Cameroon is not only firmly in the control of foreign economic dominion and in a condition of trade deficit, but had attained the status of a highly indebted poor country under the weight of a programme of state restructuring imposed on it by international financial institutions. However, in 1960, he found himself in a position to either gain autonomy within the French Union or to be independent without the support of France. Unfortunately, he opined that he was not a believer in economic independence. Though not a believer in economic independence, he had pledged during the 4th congress of the *Union Camerounaise* (UC) political party in July 1962, to address himself resolutely to the task of economic development. This pledge of his could only have fallen in line with his ambition to raise Cameroon to the status of a modern economic nation, an economic nation. By that, he actually meant helping Europeans in their mission to invade and to destroy Cameroon in the course of recycling their capital.

This eventually affected his flirtation with the concept of African socialism, which he announced during the same UC congress mentioned above. Although the concept of African socialism, which became the political slogan for his nation-building project in Cameroon, the application of which he said was to cut Cameroon clean from the anarchy and the injustices that are inherent in classical capitalism, it was stillborn. On July 10, 1965 at a UC meeting in Douala, he announced a new economic model he called planned liberalism. This new economic model Ahmadou Ahidjo was to assure profitability for private investment regardless of whether it was foreign or Cameroonian completely killed African socialism. From the day Ahmadou Ahidjo announced planned liberalism, African socialism was never heard of again.

It should be recalled that upon his accession to power (or appointment) as Prime Minister of East Cameroon in 1958, he placed as top priority on his agenda in collaboration with France, a plan to eliminate the leaders of the UPC national liberation movement, which he saw as engendering disorder. It was easy for France to have fallen for Ahmadou Ahidjo's top priority political agenda because France had failed to force the UPC leaders to adopt a pro-French political idea, as did Houphouet-Boigny and Senghor in 1950 in what was called *repli-strategique*. Just for the record, in adopting repli-*strategique* in 1950, Houphouet-Boigny and Senghor renounced the cause of nationalism (Joseph 1974:436). In his quest to become a French overseas estate manager, Ahmadou Ahidjo had to follow suit and succeeded. As a French estate manager, Ahmadou Ahidjo established for Cameroon a power structure that bordered on the dehumanisation of Cameroonians with economic consequences being trade deficit.

Ahmadou Ahidjo's Political Programme

Soaked to the skin in the French economic-loaded political philosophy, the main item on Ahmadou Ahidjo's political menu was national unity, which was a euphemism for the establishment of a police state in Cameroon. His purpose of establishing a police state in Cameroon was to create a power structure that will enable him to rule over Cameroonians aristocratically with the use of force. Seen through another lens, his political game plan was to achieve peace through military might. This game plan of his was backed by France with whom he had signed a military co-operation agreement in 1960. For that reason, no cock had to crow in Ahmadou Ahidjo's Cameroon. Having acceded to his position as a representative of his metropolitan patrons and mentors, groomed within Dr. Aujoulat's BDC, he found it incumbent on him to declare war against acts that could engender his strife to have total control over Cameroonians on behalf of his metropolitan masters. This distrustful game plan of Ahmadou Ahidjo and his metropolitan backers to have total control over Cameroonians could be achieve at that time because at the time segments of the Cameroonian society had already been polarised by the Europeans in collaboration with their local representatives in their fight against peace, freedom and emancipation. So we see that politically, Ahmadou Ahidjo sought to achieve the exact opposite of what Um Nyobe and the UPC nationalist movement had incarnated before being forced into illegality and then exterminated by the French and their allies.

After introducing what Bayart (1980:120)calls "ethic of unity" he dedicated his whole political career to establishing order through military repression under the guise of achieving unity, peace, and progress; three cardinal values that runs through most of his speeches and political writings. He sought to establish unity, peace and progress with the same intensity of force with which he had used in suppressing the UPC national liberation movement as a prerequisite in maintaining a firm hegemonic control over Cameroonians. He denied and suppressed difference with the same intensity of force as during the direct French military oppressive power. His desire to consolidate his political power thus demanded that he should create an establishment where he will have no rivalry; where no other cock will "crow" in the land but him.

In a press conference on July 2, 1963, he was unequivocal about his intention to establishing a police state as the basis of achieving this hegemonic control over Cameroonians for the global imperial order to have their way in Cameroon. In a military tone, he firmly announced that; "Henceforth, the same degree of gravity is recognised in acts which menace the national institutions as infractions committed against the security of the state." Following that press conference, he promulgated into force a draconian law No. 60 PJL-ANF of 1963, which virtually abolished all groups and associations and all sheds of opinion in the country and brought Cameroon under a state of emergency. This established powers in the office of the President of the Republic and its antennas, the CNU party, and all the instruments of state power such as the Army, Gendarmerie, and the Military Tribunals. To him the state was the only guarantor of life and property within the territorial boundaries and of ensuring foreign protection (Ahidjo 1964: 24; Ahidjo 1968: 43).Persons, communities and all social strata were expected to abandon all primordial loyalties and submit to the imposing will of the European superimposed secular state which they must look up to as the giver and guarantor of life.

President Ahmadou Ahidjo saw the UPC shadow in everybody and in every form of association or ethno-regional groupings he saw a potential base for the resurgence of the UPC liberation insurrection. According to him, if people were allowed to freely associate that can hamper the unity and peace he was out to establish as a prerequisite for achieving progress. Ahmadou Ahidjo's police state in Cameroon needed acquiescent people who must conform to the public will for no individual is of his/her own but a part of the collective will. In line with this view of things, Ahmadou Ahidjo stated that the surrender and fusion of individual liberty into the collective liberty was paramount for the political survival of the new nation (Ahidjo 1968: 89). "Divergence, therefore, in whatever form was a source of danger to the life of the young nation," declared Ahidjo in Ahidjo (1968). Consequently, he wished away the ethnic groups because, national unity means that in the course of nation-building, "there is no Ewondo, no Douala, no Bassa, no Bamileke, no Boulou, no Foulbe, but Cameroonians who see themselves everywhere as first of all being Cameroonians as long as they respected the rights of others". As he said, "there was need to build a truly united Cameroon with traditional authorities playing a fundamental role". (Ahidjo 1964: 29).in view of the fact that Ahmadou Ahidjo had thrown the post-World War II concept of national liberation to the dogs, it is obvious that when he propounded the notion of the individual conceding his liberty for the thriving of the collective liberty, he did not mean to say he was rallying Cameroonians under one stream of political consciousness to fight against foreign invasion. This can only be seen as falling in line with his drive to create a police state in Cameroon.

In his drive to create a police state in Cameroon, even multi-partyism was perceived to be a source of instability because even the constitutions of what he called 'older democracies' did not provide room for that (Ahidjo 1968: 53). He holds September 1, 1968 in high esteem as a great day the people of Cameroon decided to abolish multi-partyism and to create the one national party, the CNU, which he says was in conformity with the aspirations of the people of Cameroon to establish unity among themselves (Ahidjo 1976: 17). Defining the role of the party in achieving this task, he says it was to "foster the spirit of camaraderie" (Ahidjo 1964: 28)

In his drive to have total control over all Cameroonians, his political gimmicks included efforts to return Cameroon to its pre-1919 geographical status. This was not to be done as a strategy to extricate Cameroon from the stranglehold of imperialism but, quite on the contrary, as a strategy to establish close ties with it by subjecting a larger number people under its influence, for his political gain. Wishing to see all Cameroonians united under his firm grip as a booster to his political ambitions, he regretted the outcome of the 1961 plebiscite in which Cameroon lost part of its northern territory to Nigeria. Ahidjo

(1964: 21). To achieve success in his political gimmicks, which consisted essentially of subjecting a united Cameroon under imperial domination, he decided to echo the political views of the UPC. If Ahmadou Ahidjo decided to boom the political views of the UPC, it was not because he intended to implement them but because he intended to use it as a smokescreen to mislead Cameroonians into believing that Cameroon had achieved independence. It was in fact just an attention-grabber that was adopted by Ahmadou Ahidjo. If Ahmadou Ahidjo decided to resonate the political views of the UPC, it was not because he intended to implement it but because he intended to use it to browbeat Cameroonians into submission so he could impose his will on them. Ahmadou Ahidjo was echoing the political views of the UPC rather as a currency to buy the support of Cameroonians. At the end of the day, Ahmadou Ahidjo's booming of the political views of the UPC, however, gave him a semblance of legitimacy and made him to consolidate his position as the president of the Republic. He had in fact succeeded in deceiving Cameroonians that they had achieved independence.

Bidding to co-opt Cameroonians into the mentality of dependence after having deceived them that independence has been achieved, he covertly proclaim the role neo-colonial institutions were going to play in the perpetuation of the police state he had put in place, To that effect, he announced at a ceremony for the award of diplomas at ENAM (*Ecole Nationale d'Administration et de Magistrature*) in 1967 that the administrative cadres were going to play a decisive role within the administrative set up. In the absence of a dynamic private sector and in his bid to impose a public service mentality on Cameroonians, he said the administration was going to be the motor of development action in all domains because the administrative cadres constituted the country's intellectual capital. Surprisingly, he made it known to Cameroonians for the first time that at the head of the administrative and political realm of the nation-state was to be found the President and a

Vice President who were to be elected by a universal suffrage on the same platform. Notwithstanding the police state he had set up, President Ahmadou Ahidjo unexpectedly announced a political plan to create a Federal house of assembly. But quite contrary to the principles of parliamentary democracy in which the executive arm of government is responsible to the legislative arm of government, the federal house of assembly Ahmadou Ahidjo was to put in place was to be answerable to the Executive organ of the State, which could dissolve it in consultation with the Prime Minister (Ahidjo 1964: 25).

As far as this federal house of assembly was concerned, he said there were going to be two assemblies for the two federal states. He disclosed that this was going to be according to the provisions of the constitution, according to which there were going to be 40 parliamentarians elected into the East Cameroon's house of assembly and 10 into the West Cameroon's house of assembly. In this arrangement, the dominant position of the President of the Republic was to balance the powers of the two halves of the state. According to Ahmadou Ahidjo's political plan, this was a way of achieving the much-cherished national unity. In accordance with his Unitarian vision for Cameroon, the two territorial assemblies became the national assembly following the obliteration of the federal structures in 1972. In addition to that but still in accordance with his Unitarian political plan, Ahmadou Ahidjo put up the idea that there was great need for a certain amount of ethnic and political balance because political order was a condition *sine qua non* for the unity of spirit, the unity of patriotic sentiments which should all amount to a single stream of national consciousness (Ahidjo ibid.).

As far as foreign affairs were concerned, President Ahmadou Ahidjo took his Unitarian political plan for Cameroon into international politics. Expanding his Unitarian vision for Cameroon into international politics, he held the view that," the civilisation of the 20th century was characterised by the unity of Africa and the unity of the diverse people of the world but within the non-aligned agreement" (Ahidjo 1976:121). Cameron's diplomacy, therefore, while taking into account the peculiarity of the country, addressed itself to international problems. It was based on his desire, which was part of the wishes of his metropolitan backers, to expand his Unitarian vision for Cameroon into international politics that President Ahmadou Ahidjo participated in the creation of sub regional and regional organisations (Ahidjo ibid: 37) under the designs and directives of the European powers as a strategy of hemming in more African countries into economic zones. This resulted in the creation of UDEAC the post-colonial contraption that became CEMAC, with a central bank and currency controlled from Paris.

In line with the post-war modernisation theory, which was an antithetical antidote to the independent struggles, embodied in the notion of development in which European countries were to embark on sponsoring projects in post-colonial societies with the intention of transforming them into neo-Europes, Ahmadou Ahidjo completely ignored the possibility of developing an indigenous economic model and so depended totally on international corporations for project realisation leaving a particular pride of place to Europe. He had made these intentions clear through an announcement he made at the 4th UC congress of July 4 – 8, 1962. At the 5th congress of the UC party of November 30, 1965 he announced that the fruits of his co-operation with foreign governments were there for all to see. He praised the ceaseless efforts of France for its generous assistance to Cameroon, which he said concretised the bonds of friendship between France and his government. Bidding to cajole more foreign participation, he also thanked the United States of America for the Kumba-Mamfe road, the Federal Republic of Germany for the Mora-Fort Foureau road, etc. Counting dependence as a blessing, Ahmadou Ahidjo said the realisation of these projects were indications that dependence for foreign assistance in the nation-building project was beginning to bear fruits. Regrettably, these projects, in reality only succeeded in misleading Cameroonians into believing that they could depend largely on European countries for their infrastructural development, a perception that completely killed the national liberation struggle and established dependence as a development trajectory.

The Foundation Philosophy of Ahmadou Ahidjo's Economic Programme

President Ahmadou Ahidjo's economic programme for nation-building in Cameroon was intricately linked to his political agenda, which was externally oriented; to meet foreign economic interests, based on the economy of the market with a major focus towards dependence on foreign sources (Ahidjo 1964: 55), but which was not separated from the political realm of the state. This economic model of Ahmadou Ahidjo had its foundation philosophy in the political idea wherein the state is a business enterprise run in partnership with European countries and foreign financial organisations. This was, without a doubt, derived from the prevailing post-colonial thought of immediate post-independence era in Africa according to which "superior" Europe was the "giver" of development to the "inferior" people of the world including the people of Africa. It was at the 4th UC Congress of July 4–8, 1962 at Ebolowa that Ahmadou Ahidjo had made known his economic programme for Cameroon according to which the state was a business enterprise that does business with its foreign partners with the fallouts being development. In that congress, he made it known that;

> "We have chosen to carry our economic and social development within a liberally planned framework; that is to say within a system of liberty, within which private, national and foreign enterprise work together; a system of development in which, the State has not only interest, but which it plans, a system of development which presupposes that the State, with a view to creating new industries and

enterprises, … not only gives its consent but participates actively".

Within this politico-economic framework, his intentions were to ensure regional balance by redistributing the fruits of this business enterprise throughout the region in a way as to double the living standards of Cameroonians in twenty years. To achieve his ambition, he targeted the agricultural sector, road infrastructure and the industrial sector, which consisted mainly of modernising agriculture and the pursuit of industrial development and the purchase of equipment from foreign countries distributing them throughout the national territory in a manner that will keep the regions at equilibrium which thus hopefully brining about a strong national imagination (Ahidjo 1976: 33). In the domain of agriculture, he launched the campaign for Green Revolution. Green Revolution was to embody all the different departments that are involved in the agricultural production sector intended to achieve better production results and ensure food security. All of these were to occur within the Cameroon plan of 1960 that he announced in Douala on October 9, 1963.

To this effect, he planned to convert and exploit the colonial infrastructure and the economic ground-work it entailed (agriculture, staff, economic and administrative organisation, roads, telecommunications, ports etc.,) and to focus on training, to encourage initiative, to increase and diversify production, to develop small and medium size industries, as well as to pursue and diversify foreign partners, since he said he did not believe in economic independence (see his speeches at the 4th UC congress of July 4 – 8, 1962 and that of October 9, 1963). Based on his political views of a state as being a business enterprise that does business with its foreign partners resulting in handouts that amount to development, his economic programme was externally oriented. Though not a believer in economic independence, he wished to see a sound financial policy that will lead to national self-financing.

In the domain of road infrastructure and subject to his political view of unifying the entire national territory to his benefit in particular and that of the metropolitan economy in general, the government was to embark on the construction of a Trans-Cameroon road network that was to link the north of the country to the south (Ahidjo 1964: 55). He said this will facilitate economic activities within the new state as a precondition to facilitating economic gravitation towards Europe. In the domain of investment, he previewed the sum of FCFA 10 billion out of which aid from external sources, notably from the *Fonds d'Aide et de la Coopération* (FAC), friendly nations, FEDOM, was to constitute 72 percent while internal public financing was to make up for the rest but with a progressive reduction on the taxation on foreign investment as a measure to attract foreign partners. As if he had forgotten that he does not belief in economic independence, he also planned to take steps to catalyse internal efforts towards reducing heavy dependence on foreign capital (Ahidjo ibid: 56).

Unfortunately, before President Ahmadou Ahidjo's externally oriented economy could reach his 20 years economic growth target, it was hit by a global inflation and the rise in petrol prices. That international economic mishap in fact greatly destabilised Cameroon's economy since it was intractably linked to the global economy. Consequently, the country witnessed a drop in its GDP from 8 percent in 1970 to 4 percent in 1971 and further to 3 percent in 1972, but according to him, government had taken precautionary measures to avoid a drastic drop in the standards of living of the population (Ahidjo 1976: 32). The worsening international and economic crisis prompted President Ahmadou Ahidjo to backpedal, eventually announcing what he called self-centred development. His belated idea of self-centred development consisted mainly of mobilising national resources and energies for development, thus making people the motor of development (Ahidjo 1976: 165), towards achieving what he tardily called self-decolonisation (Ahidjo 1964:121).

His belated economic plan along these lines was to make credits available as much as possible for local initiatives and investments. While announcing the Cameroon plan in Douala on October 9, 1963, he announced the creation of diverse bodies and committees among which were the Intergovernmental Committee for the Plan and Economic Development, the National Technical Committee for Economic Reconversion and General Orientation of Co-operation, the National Investment Corporation, the Rural Development Fund, etc. All these, he said, were to combine efforts with those of the Economic and Social Council, the National Credit Council, the Cameroon Development Bank, and the Chamber of Commerce in responding to the problem of what he described as underdevelopment.

Pushing forward with his belated economic plan, Ahmadou Ahidjo announced at a UC meeting in Douala on July 10, 1965, the adoption of planned liberalism as an economic model for his regime. And on July 10, 1966, while delivering an address at the Federal Advance School of Agriculture, he announced that in spite of efforts made at industrialisation, Cameroon was going to remain a predominantly an agricultural country where the country will derive most of its resources while at the same time improving the standards of living of the 85 percent of those living in the rural areas who are engaged mainly in agriculture. This was an emphasis and a follow up to the second five-year plan, a large part of which was devoted to agriculture. In line with his efforts to retool his belated economic plan through agriculture, he had also announced that he intends to strengthen and to increase the number of co-operative movements and to train the technical personnel in the co-operative field who would be able to apply the principles of communalism as a key strategy to agricultural development. See his Investiture Speech of January 18, 1958, and his speech of January 11, 1965 in Doumé. Inadvertently, this was based on the realisation that there was need for the population to participate in the subordination of Cameroon's economy to that of Europe as he elaborated in his speech at the 4th UC Congress of July 4-8, 1962 in which he stated that:

> "Abandoning the population to themselves is fraught with disastrous economic and political consequences. We reject all organisations of a collective type; but we think that it is necessary to organise and to control, by the use of democratic procedure, the active participation of the population in the development of our country".

Surprisingly, in the overall appraisal of Cameroon's economy, President Ahmadou Ahidjo himself regretted that foreign investment and its attachment of Cameroon's economy to the market oriented global economy, like its *third world* counterparts, was working negatively for the country's economy (Ahidjo 1976: 166).And during the 3rd UC Party Congress of September 1960 he pointed out that:

> "To analyse rapidly the impediments which have delayed or hindered the take-off of the Cameroon economy, one has only in fact to cite:
> 1) The functioning of the international exchange system as a result of which Cameroon and other staple product countries have found themselves in an extremely weak negotiating position and the direct consequence of this state of affairs is that Cameroon is faced [with] ever worsening terms of trade;
> 2) The production of exportable goods is largely due to capital of foreign origin. The corresponding profits are not used for internal development because they are immediately repatriated to the countries of origin of the investors.
> 3) The rapidity with which the conquests of progress has taken root in Cameroon before the establishment of economic conditions, entailing extremely costly measure of social legislation, an administrative infrastructure, luxury spending, and the development of social equipment (sic);

4) The absence of aid to progress, such as the accumulation of capital, the spread of techniques, the adaptation of institutions, vocational training, voluntary or compulsory savings;

5) The lack of encouragement to invest as a result of the feeble purchasing power, which arises, to paraphrase a famous economist, from the low revenue, resulting from low productivity which in turn, is a result of inadequate incentive to invest".

Though no country in the world can develop like a monad, cut off from the rest of the world, it should be noted that as early as 1960, President Ahmadou Ahidjo could realise by himself the adverse effects of international capital on an externally oriented economy. His observation in fact highlights the evils that are inbuilt in dependent economies. In Cameroon today, over half a century after former president Ahmadou Ahidjo, who was not a believer in economic independence, observed the dangers of dependent economies, the situation today actually shows that a rigorous pursuit of international capital by the two successive regimes in Cameroon has not proved to be the best development trajectory. Further than what former president Ahmadou Ahidjo observed in 1960,Cameroon has moved from the status of a poor country as assessed by the French aggressors in 1946 (Wonyu 1988) to the status of a heavily indebted poor country as assessed by the IMF/World Bank Breton Woods twins in 2001. This was after the Breton woods twins had imposed the Poverty Reduction Facility Growth (PRFG) in 1999. The 1999 Poverty Reduction Facility Growth (PRFG), which was spelled out in the Poverty Reduction Strategy Paper (PRSP), was a mechanism that was developed by the Biya regime to be used as an application for admission into the decision point of the HIPC by the IMF/World Bank. In other words, the PRSP was a mechanism that was developed by a regime to combat the adverse effects of international financial agencies on a dependent economy.

However, having decided not to "abandon the population to themselves" but to involve the "active participation of the population in the development of our country", Ahmadou Ahidjo and his metropolitan mentors came up with an innovative idea, which was the famous Green Revolution. Green Revolution summarised Ahmadou Ahidjo's much talked about agricultural policy and turned the attention of Cameroonians to food production. Typical of development programmes that are implemented in dependent economies with a latent intention to serve metropolitan needs, Green Revolution undoubtedly yielded positive results for Cameroon in terms of food security, but it's down side was equally devastating. Green Revolution gave the French and their other European allies the leeway to take control of the other (vital) sectors of the economy such as the exploration, exploitation, and the exportation of oil (black gold), and heavy investments in commerce and industry. To realise his much cherished agricultural policy, between 1962 and 1975 a multiplicity of agro-industrial concerns cropped up. These included SEMRY, SODERIM, SOCAPALM, HEVECAM, CENEEMA, ZAPI-Est, SODEBLE, SODECAO, MIDEVIV, ONAREST, SODEPA, CDC, *Office national de participation au développement, Société Camerounaise des tabacs, Office céréalier, Opération Yabassi-Bafang*, OCB, etc. To crown it all, a rural development fund (FONADER) was established in 1973, regional schools of agriculture were opened, and farmers were mobilised through the frequent organisation of agro-pastoral shows that drew popular enthusiasm to food production and left the French alone in the extraction of oil from the Cameroon coastline.

A combine effect of plenty of food and money paid as salaries to civil servants and workers of public and para-public corporations plus plenty of beer and women completely crippled the ability of Cameroonians to think of reconstituting themselves into a revolutionary force against the white man's thievery and destruction of Cameroon. In consequence, as Cameroonians concentrated in food production, Ahmadou

Ahidjo's metropolitan partners in crime looted the mineral wealth of the land with impunity. In the mind of Cameroonians food, money, beer and women, was the "life" they have been dreaming about. To them, independence had yielded fruits for them to enjoy. While Cameroonians revelled in their new found post-independence life, enjoying what they mistook for the fruits of independence, the French, Americans, the Israelis and other Europeans were busy extracting petrol from the Cameroon coastline. The French oil company SEREPCA (*Société des études, de recherches et d'exploitation pétrolière du Cameroun*), inaugurated in 1954 at the Wouri estuary by the French governor Soucadaux in the presence of Cameroonians like Arouna Njoya and Soppo Priso and the notorious French man Dr. Louis-Paul Aujoulat, was able to repatriate a profit of over FCFA 4.7 billion to France within six years, i.e.in 1960. To make sure that the distraction was total Ahmadou Ahidjo chose to lunch his "Green Revolution" programme in Buea on March 9, 1973. The choice of Buea for the lunch of the Green Revolution was not by chance. Buea was and still is the headquarters of the region where the oil extracting activities were intense. No Cameroonian could suspect this thievery strategy put in place by the European pirates executed by Ahmadou Ahidjo who told Cameroonians in 1980, for the first time at the Bafoussam Congress of the CNU party that plans for the exploiting of oil in Cameroon were underway. Ahmadou Ahidjo's announcement at the Bafoussam Congress of the CNU rather contradicted his earlier announcement of a drop in the GDP between 1970 and 1972, which was, paradoxically, the peak period of oil extraction in Cameroon. In any case, the decline in the oil extraction directly affected Cameroon's economy adversely in the sense that the oil extraction was not and has never been done by Cameroonians for Cameroonians. It was done by Europeans for their market with Cameroon and Cameroonians being only an appendage of that huge global market from where they buy what is extracted from their own soil at exorbitant prices.

Ahmadou Ahidjo's Social Programme

President Ahmadou Ahidjo's social programme was also a direct consequence of his political agenda in which he conceived the social welfare of "inferior" people as being depended on the social systems of the "superior" Europeans. He therefore tailored his social programme to benefit from the "solidarity and combined efforts of humanity" in what he termed to be an "interdependent world social system." In designing his social programme in this way, Ahmadou Ahidjo did not take into consideration the international injustices with hideous and tragic consequences which have resulted in the imbalances that have provoked poverty in Asia, Africa, and Latin America. Ahmadou Ahidjo's social programme rolled out amid intense mineral extractive activities that were going on in Cameroon unknown to Cameroonians. His social programme seemed to have been carefully tailored to render Cameroonians apathetic to the overwhelming economic piracy that was going on under his supervision. Consequently, besides considering education, health and the social services as agencies of social and economic development, he also intended a labour code to be the catalysing instrument for social progress as he puts it. (Ahidjo 1964: 90). Unfortunately, the labour code that Ahmadou Ahidjo's social programme produced for Cameroonians instead ironically granted Europeans the muscle to have an economic stranglehold on Cameroon as Ngwasiri (1997: 41) observed.

In the domain of education, which he considered as a social phenomenon in its role of imparting physical, intellectual and moral values in the individual that are requisites for the political order, he envisaged education (Western education) as a primordial necessity in a society such as Cameroon that was in transition, from its "inferior" status to a "superior" one. For that reason, he intended to make education available to all at all levels, including scientific research and knowledge transfer, from the society of "superior" people to that of "inferior" people. To him, this was an essential domain for human investment with eventual social capital accruing from it for the benefit of the development of Cameroon that was positioning itself within a globalising world, and also as a dynamic force for social stratification (Ahidjo ibid: 91; Ahidjo 1976: 79). At the 4th UC congress that held in Ebolowa from July 4–8, 196, he obtrusively maintained that; "the education policy should be necessarily linked with the employment policy," stating that there was no use training specialists if there was no possibility of using their skills without delay. There arose a need to develop a system of scientific and technical education as an indispensable aspect of Cameroon. While observing that Reunification brought together two systems of education with their peculiarities (Ahidjo 1964: 98), he also noted that both Western education and employment in Cameroon have always been inexorably linked to the political-economic exigencies of European countries.

In the domain of health, he stressed that health is an essential domain that would ensure human well-being because it will eliminate disease. He pointed out that the benefit of a good health system is that it will provide the political realm with a strong and healthy human capital necessary for the task of nation-building. He went further than that to put plans afoot for the establishment of health infrastructure in all the regions of the country (Ahidjo ibid: 16; Ahidjo 1976: 88).

With regards to the improvement in the condition of workers in the country, a labour code was established. And for the general amelioration of living standards both in the rural and urban areas, plans for water supply, the provision of electricity, and housing scheme under SIC, was previewed (Ahidjo 1976: 89) although this was never achieved at the time he resigned as president of the republic. In the overall evaluation of Ahidjo's social programme, it can be said that it was a social programme that was something of a kind of a corporate social responsibility in the sense that it was geared towards making Cameroonians to feel at ease as much as possible, enough food, enough money, enough beer, free health care, free education, etc., while the Europeans continued with their economic robbery of the land.

It was also a social programme that was tailored as a cold war strategy, which could explain why it declined after the end of the cold war.

Ahidjo's Cultural Programme

The cultural programme for President Ahmadou Ahidjo, which was based on the reinforcement and the facilitation of the spread of Western education as implanted in Cameroon by the French and the British, implied that the culture of the "inferior", indigenous people of Cameroon has become meaningless. Thus the inferior people will have to move from their "inferior" status to a superior" one. Education in Cameroon was to be based on the two colonial cultural heritages of France and Great Britain. According to Ahmadou Ahidjo, this Eurocentric education would be adapted to meet local reality while still responding to global exigencies (Ahidjo 1964: 97). , He envisioned the use of the media in the implantation of Western immature notions of Enlightenment noting, however, that the present system of education corresponded neither to the African realities nor to the status of an independent country in a century that was characterised by a dire need for technical and economic development (Ahidjo 1964: 25). He saw the need to study the social and communal traits of the African culture for the reinforcement of African unity (Ahidjo ibid). To the extent that he had the will and occasion to reinforce African unity it was only as an apology to the indigenous cultural system. Ahidjo's cultural programme targeted the indigenous culture for destruction in order to establish a floating culture that benefited the type of state he and his European patrons had put in place.

Ahmadou Ahidjo's Strategy for Nation-Building

By strategy here we are trying to answer the question of how, in terms the techniques, Ahmadou Ahidjo was going to realise his political philosophy. Supposedly, since President Ahmadou

Ahidjo's mission was to establish a strong state with Europeans and international financial institutions as its partners, the techniques he was going to deploy to achieve that goal consisted mainly of using brute force as a strategy of guarding against any possibilities of an insurrection or a rebellion against the white man's atrocities in Cameroon where he served as local representative. According to him the 20th century was an era for planning, and all sorts of planning entailed creation, construction, instruction, education, inscribed both in space and time, needing the action of a powerful head of state whose power is felt in all domains (Ahidjo 1964: 24). It is obvious that Ahmadou Ahidjo was talking about the type of planning that leads to the subversion of the power of the Cameroonian people. He actually meant to talk about the need for a post-colonial Cameroon to have a powerful head of state capable of subjecting Cameroonians to the whims of his metropolitan partners in crime. With that in mind, Ahmadou Ahidjo sought to establish a Cameroon wherein Cameroonians toiled to make the world a better place for Ahmadou Ahidjo and his metropolitan partners in crime. To him, the most effective strategy was to adopt a presidential, one party system, that claimed to incarnate the myth and spirit of the people within a strong state. The interests of the state would subsume the interests of the "inferior" people of Cameroon who became no more important than to the "development" that was coming from the "superior" realm of the worthy European countries. The effective implementation of such a plan required an all-knowing and all-powerful president who incarnates state institutions, doing the planning and the execution without question of power-sharing or any form of opposition (Joseph 1978: 70; Kengne Pakam 1986: 21). He maintained that this kind of planning needed a strong president whose duty is to issue orders. To obey without question would become the duty of the people.

Ahmadou Ahidjo's strategy or line of attack subverted the power of the people of Cameroon and put it at his beck and call. By extension, this strategy sustained the power of his metropolitan partners in crime. The best way to achieve this power dynamic he thought, was to put in place a strong power structure in which his will and that of his metropolitan backers effectively carried out, planned and directed from abroad. That was in fact the way he thought he could realise his Unitarian vision, which was to unite the brain and muzzle of all the people of Cameroon for his benefit and by extension that of the metropolitan economy. Keeping churches aside in that endeavour, he envisioned a one Party system in which the ruling party swallowed up the will of the people under an imposed ethic of unity which denies all forms of associations and expression. An imposed ethic of unity which denies all forms of association and expression enabled Ahmadou Ahidjo, who would have the last word in the land, to do the dirty job in Cameroon for the European invaders in the name of economic planning and social provisioning. All this with the major aim of attracting foreign capital. Thus, what Um Nyobe fought to unite Cameroonians *against* Ahmadou Ahidjo fought to unite Cameroonians *for*, namely; European invasion, destruction, and the dehumanisation of the people. No doubt what President Ahidjo did was not what he wrote and whenever he tried to implement what he wrote the results were either counterproductive or simply yielded nothing for the Cameroonian people. If only these sacrifices had fetched him the much sought after foreign investment he needed to push on with his political agenda. A good example of what he implemented that obtained a counterproductive result was the imposed ethic of unity that gave a semblance of unity only to become shattered by the liberalisation laws of the early 1990s.

The loose federated structure that emerged in 1961 was not what Um Nyobe was aiming at. The Um Nyobe-led UPC wanted a unitary state in which the people united in their efforts to wipe out all traces of colonial wickedness and to establish a harmonious nation. Unfortunately, President Ahmadou Ahidjo's "ethic of unity" or "unity by the whip" fermented ethnic tensions. These tensions broke loose and degenerated into conflicts during President Paul Biya's liberalisation era causing the political base to become fragile. Although Ahmadou Ahidjo is held in popular esteem as one who had achieved an economic miracle for Cameroon, this was based on floating capital, capital that did not trickle down to the roots of the grass. With achievement based on capital that did not trickle down under unity by the whip, minority groups suppressed and maintained under the dominion of powerful ethno-regional blocs were granted positions of privilege within the post-colonial power structure under Ahmadou Ahidjo. These broke loose under Paul Biya to demand their own share of the money derived from the theft and sale of resources to Europeans in exchange for loyalty.

Unfortunately and ironically, Ahmadou Ahidjo's planned economy, which had a heavy agricultural policy orientation supported by a multiplicity of agro-industrial concerns "collapsed" easily in the face of economic crisis during the tenure of office of his successor, Paul Biya, like a column of clay. Why it collapsed so easily in the face of an economic crisis is also explained by what he himself had observed in 1960 as adverse effects of global capital on dependent economy. What president Ahmadou Ahidjo had put in place was in fact a dependent economy and as a dependent economy it became captive to international dictatorship of the World Bank bringing Cameroonians to their economic knees. Ironic yet it couldn't have resulted otherwise. Facts reveal that Ahmadou Ahidjo's nation-building idea established a territorial panorama open to his metropolitan patrons in the services of robbery and political manipulation and domination. This nation had become closed to Cameroonians who remained ignorant as to what political economy was all about.

Chapter Four

Paul Biya's New Deal Political Philosophy for Nation-Building

The unexpected resignation of Cameroon's first head of state Ahmadou Ahidjo on November 4, 1982 brought a sigh of relief to Cameroonians who wished for an end to that era of terror. Paul Biya took over the mantle of office as Cameroon's second head of state on November 6, 1982.He raised a lot of hope in the population with his New Deal slogan (Gwellem 1984). This chapter examines and describes the characteristics or content of the New Deal political philosophy. We will examine this this philosophy in order to evaluate the transition at the helm of state in Cameroon. Did this change at the helm maintain continuity of one philosophy? Was this a change of philosophy? Did this new philosopher of the nation continue to imagine the nation as if in service to Europeans on behalf of Cameroonians? Was it a change that restored the liberty of Cameroonians to think their own nation by themselves or was it merely a change of European-made political philosophers? An understanding of the New Deal political philosophy or proposed vision of society helps us understand the kind of transition that occurred at the helm of state in Cameroon in 1982. We will address is whether the new deal political philosophy for nation-building in Cameroon was a home-grown political philosophy that indicated that at last Cameroonians had arrived at a point where they have had a political philosopher who could genuinely think the nation on their behalf . Was the new deal political philosophy the mental product of yet another political philosopher who was thinking the nation in Cameroon on a European mandate, like his predecessor?

Paul Biya's New Deal Philosophy as a Neo-Ahidjoism

Whenever the word neo is used it is often used to refer to a phenomenon that has been picked up from the shelf, dusted, recycled and reused probably with the intention to achieve the same results as did its earlier version. Neo could also refer to a newer version of a certain incidence that is re-occurring in a certain context probably in a different form but which is going to achieve the same results as did its previous edition. For example, when we talk of neo-colonialism we mean to talk of colonialism re-occurring in a new form. When we talk of neo-archaism we are referring to archaic things recycled and brought anew probably for the same purpose. Thus we might talk of Paul Biya's New Deal Philosophy as the same post-colonial political ideas of Ahmadou Ahidjo recycled for re-insertion in Cameroon aimed at achieving the same objective that Ahmadou Ahidjo sought to achieve in a post-colonial context. Hence; a neo-Ahidjoism. Ntumazah (2001) even refers to Paul Biya as a replay of Ahmadou Ahidjo. It should be noted that the two men were not age mates nor were they classmates. Nevertheless, they have something in common that made the successor a re-occurrence of his predecessor. Both men occurred in Cameroon at different times, probably with different tactics which were all intended to achieve the same results; to assist the great prostitute who sits on many waters to force kings and priests to commit adultery with her. The one major indicator that points to Ahmadou Ahidjo and Paul Biya as the same breed is that both were virtually groomed by the same people who stage-managed their accession to power. One eventually succeeded the other. For example, Paul Biya, upon his return to Cameroon in October 1962, after six years of studies in France, arrived with a special recommendation letter from the same Louis-Paul Aujoulat to Ahidjo, to groom him as successor. It should be recalled that Louis-Paul Aujoulat is the same French man who politically mentored Ahmadou Ahidjo in Cameroon and stage-managed him to power. This tends to point to the fact that the New deal political philosophy is probably a neo-Ahidjoism. Two fundamental similarities between President Paul Biya and his predecessor exist 1) they both came to power without the mandate of the people of Cameroon; 2) if the Louis-Paul Aujoulat connection is a fact, then it means that both men were European-tailor-made political philosophers who were on a European assignment to think the nation in Cameroon on behalf of Cameroonians. As Mongo Beti (1978: 97) points out, this was a European strategy for continuous occupation, enslavement, exploitation and domination. While former President Ahmadou Ahidjo served as a direct representative of the French invaders, presiding over their structure of power put in place in Cameroon, Paul Biya served as a loyalist student within it under him. François Mitterrand, a socialist, did not want to continue with Ahmadou Ahidjo, because he was seen as a Gaullist relic. So he had to select Paul Biya for the job based on both his having been a loyalist *student* within the power structure the Europeans had put in place and partly because the structure of international politics was changing and needed new political actors to play a different role to rope Cameroon into the new structure of international politics that was emerging. For sure, François Mitterrand's decision to install Paul Biya in Cameroon as head of state was actually a vital ingredient for the insertion of Cameroon into the new structure of international politics emerging towards the end of communism in Socialist Russia. In other words, the structure of international politics was changing and so required a different representative in Cameroon. Could Paul Biya, therefore, have thought the nation in Cameroon differently from the way Ahmadou Ahidjo thought it?

Before we get to how the structure of international politics was changing towards the end of the Cold War subsequent to the fall of communism in Socialist Russia, it is imperative to verify the history of Paul Biya's mental development. This should lead us to the foundation of his political ideas. This will help us see why Paul Biya was going to very easily step into Ahmadou Ahidjo's shoes. Why Paul Biya and not someone else?

A journey into the process through which he came to know what he knew on which his political ideas developed and depended is a major step towards answering the question of why it was going to be Paul Biya and not someone else. This exercise is based on the hypothesis that people act according to the knowledge they have. Paul Biya studied in France. Upon his return to Cameroon in 1962 he came with a special recommendation letter to his would be predecessor. This clearly indicates a scheme to ensure continuity. But why Paul Biya of all? What kind of political ideas had he been exposed to that could have qualified him to have very easily stepped into Ahmadou Ahidjo's political shoes? Was he the most educated Cameroonian at the time or was he the most politically active Cameroonian at the time? If none of the above attributes qualified him then the French intrigues as we will discover later on in the course of this analysis must have favoured him for a reason best known only by France. Whatever the case, brief background knowledge of the man will almost certainly open our eyes.

Paul Biya, whose father was a catechist with the French Roman Catholic mission, introduced in the south of Cameroon by the French, was born in February 13, 1933 in Mvomeka in the south of Cameroon. His early childhood years of schooling in the catholic primary school in his native south, secondary and high school in Lycée Leclerc in Yaoundé must have completely starved him of the social realities of the Bulu people, his ancestral roots. In his bid to become a priest, he continued with his formal education at the catholic major seminary at Akono in the south. To make matters worse, instead of becoming a priest, after the major seminary, he proceeded to Paris where he was trained at the *Institut des Hautes Études d' Outre-merde* Paris. This institute trained Managers of French overseas territories.. Here, Paul Biya was completely frenchified and made ready to serve France in Cameroon to the best of his abilities.

Like most contemporary Cameroonian youths, the young and yet innocent Paul Biya was victimised by systematically famishing him of the knowledge and the world view of his roots.

These roots were completely ripped out and foreign ones grafted in a process which only stimulated and incited his responses to the sensory perceptions of post-colonialism. He was subjected to an uncritical and prejudicial belief in the fleeting illusions of post-colonialism according to which modernity is held to be the only development trajectory, with no alternative. This not only hybridised him but actually un-Africanised him as well. Hence, Paul Biya grew up like a hybridized and bourgeoisified child whose passion for life was fired by the illusions of post-colonialism, closely associated with the French culture in particular and modernity in general. Tinged with the ideology of hegemonic dominance he had imbibed during his early upbringing years of schooling in Western educational institutions, he was completely bereft of rational thoughts. This must have armed him with the post-colonial idea that Africa's *development* depended on France in particular and on the West in general. This was also reinforced by the positivist view of Africa at the time according to which Africa must depend on the West for all what it materially needs to develop. To be sure that he better served the interests of France in Cameroon, he had to be avoided from getting in touch with reality, which could reclaim him. And so upon his return from Paris in October 1962 at the age of 29, dripping wet with a passion for modernity as the only development trajectory available to man on earth, he was strategically placed at the presidency of the Republic, first as *Chargé de Mission*, Director of Civil Cabinet, and then as Secretary General, directly under the "supervision" of his would-be predecessor Ahmadou Ahidjo, a French puppet. Having never sweated in the streets of Yaoundé doing menial jobs to survive or looking for an employment opportunity to experience what an ordinary Cameroonian youth of his age would experience. Effortlessly and without any precedence or exposure to the daily actualities of life in Cameroon, Paul Biya became the Prime Minister of Cameroon in 1975. As Prime Minister, the road to becoming the president of the Republic was paved from behind the scenes by the very France that had put in place the necessary conditions that stimulated his taste for things French and the oblivious desire to participate in the French enterprise for economic looting Cameroon. Prior to Paul Biya becoming prime Minister, in February 1975, during the CNU Congress of "maturity" in Douala, President Ahmadou Ahidjo, announced the creation of the post of Prime Minister. This must have been a strategy to circumvent the succession of S. T Muna, an Anglophone, who was then president of the National Assembly with constitutional rights to succession in case of a vacancy. The President of the Republic's announcement of the creation of the post of prime minister prompted a revision of the constitution. Eventually, on May 9, 1975, the post of Prime Minister was created. On June 30th Ahidjo appointed Paul Biya Prime Minister, a process that seems to have been planned by France twenty years earlier. Finally, on June 29th, 1979 the constitution was revised to make Paul Biya Prime Minister with rights to succession.

This constitutional revision tactically placing Paul Biya on a path to constitutionally succeeding Ahmadou Ahidjo as president was followed in 1977 by an offstage manoeuvre of Giscard d'Estaing then the president of France. According to the political chase game of Giscard d'Estaing, the presidents of the French post-colonial states in Africa were old and so needed replacement. Those earmarked for replacement were Sedar Senghor of Senegal, Houphouet-Boigny of Cote d'Ivoire, and Ahmadou Ahidjo of Cameroon. Although in the case of Cameroon Ahmadou Ahidjo was not very old as such, there was need to replace him because, according to the French political logic, he had started "thinking Cameroonian", becoming suspect. President Ahmadou Ahidjo's predicaments started in 1975 when the French realised, to their dismay that he was trying to put in place some national projects to the dislike of the French who suspected that he may "get out of French control." Overestimating himself and taking the French for granted, between 1970 and 1975, Ahmadou Ahidjo had, for example, backed out of *Air Afrique,* which was created and controlled by

France, to create CAMAIR on July 26, 1971 as a purely indigenous airline company. He had also attempted to revise the 1961 Franco-Cameroon cultural accord. These two major moves by Ahmadou Ahidjo infuriated France and brought about the French plan for his "dethronement". Dethroning Ahmadou Ahidjo meant France had to foist someone else at the helm of the Cameroon state. This person must be a French loyalist who is faithful to ensure that Cameroon remains under the influence and dominion of France.

Realising that the project for the continuous domination of Cameroon by France was realisable through the constitution, the French had to make a choice between Ayissi Mvodo, Sengat Kuoh, and Paul Biya. But Giscard d'Estaing preferred Paul Biya because the French found him the most docile of all. To ensure the smooth implementation of the French plan for succession in Cameroon, the constitution had to eliminate possible "aspirants to the throne" including S. T. Muna then president of the National Assembly and constitutional successor. That paved the way for the successor of Ahmadou Ahidjo to be put in place constitutionally. And Paul Biya, who was also politically groomed by the same French men who had groomed Ahmadou Ahidjo such as Louis-Paul Aujoulat, Roland Pré, and Robert Delavignette, in 1975, became Prime Minister. Consistent with French designs to foist Paul Biya at the helm, the revised constitution of June 29, 1979 made him constitutional successor of Ahmadou Ahidjo. On November 4, 1982 Ahmadou Ahidjo resigned suddenly after a return from France just a day before Paul Biya stepped into his shoes as the constitutional successor. The most surprising thing about Ahmadou Ahidjo's abrupt resignation is that it occurred barely two years after he had triumphed in the 1980 election by a crushing 99.99% of the total votes cast. Paul Biya finally became the second president of Cameroon, inaugurated on November 6, 1982.

As a Cameroonian of the old generation of politicians, Paul Biya's name does not appear anywhere as having participated in the political activities that marked the post-world War II era in

Africa in general and in Cameroon in particular. This leaves us with Communal Liberalism as the only option of accessing his political philosophy. Communal Liberalism is taken to be Paul Biya's political blue print for Cameroon because, as a book, it largely reflects his mental disposition and places him in the category of the philosophers of the nation in Cameroon. From his views in Communal Liberalism, it is not surprising that he could never have been opposed to the French in particular who psychologically groomed him. Europeans he considered, like his predecessor, as source of the money required for "nation-building". He must collaborate even if this means enslaving Cameroonians in the process.

As a result, Paul Biya, like Ahmadou Ahidjo, ruled Cameroon in collaboration with the international financial institutions whose money he badly needs for his development projects. He outlined these projects in his famous Cameroon vision 2035. Both communal liberalism and vision 2035 published in 2009 demonstrate that Paul Biya, like his predecessor, fully imbedded the logic of international financial institutions hook, line and sinker. Implanting his programmes in Cameroon as well as European tailor-made programmes in Cameroon in the name of development became his mission (see the signing of the corporation accord with the European Union, for example). While President Ahmadou Ahidjo's Plan Liberalism was tailor-made by France for her overseas captive territories, President Paul Biya's New Deal political philosophy, expressed in Communal Liberalism, reveals its inspiration from a foreign source. The political philosophy failed to appropriately adapt to the situation on the ground and so could not achieve for Cameroon and its people what the new deal political philosopher had in mind. A closer look at the New Deal political philosophy reveals that it was in fact a transposed and maladapted version of President Franklin D. Roosevelt's social and economic programme for the USA from 1934 to 1940. For one thing, Communal Liberalism resembles President, Franklin Roosevelt's New Deal social and economic programme. In the

USA, the application of Franklin Roosevelt's New Deal devalued the dollar by 40 per cent, the application of the New Deal in Cameroon devalued the FCFA by 50 per cent, with the crippling effect of doubling interest rates for foreign debts. Roosevelt's New Deal brought about the expansion of business in the USA. However, in the USA this failed to lower unemployment. Paul Biya's New Deal led to business expansion as well because it liberalised the political realm facilitating the invasion of the economic base by foreign business. This travesty of business expansion dispossessed Cameroonians and enriched European countries. Paul Biya's New Deal like the original version of Franklin Roosevelt contained a semblance of a socialist programme but were in fact capitalist in essence (also see Lovett Z. Elango 1988: 1cies 60,161). Ahmadou Ahidjo and Paul Biya were mercenaries in the hands of international financial agencies and European countries for the enslavement of Cameroonians under the ploy of bringing development.

Now that we have examined the psychological factors that might have facilitated Paul Biya's susceptibility to foreign social and economic policy now turn to an exploration of the political factors that might have smoothened his path to progress. Paul Biya came to power towards the end of the cold war when the USA had abandoned the politics of isolationism and commenced to assert its leadership role in the imperialist camp. At this time, it becomes clear that for Paul Biya appropriately imbibed the New Deal philosophy to look legitimate within the circles of international politics. At this juncture within this new the structure of international politicking, it was but predictable for Paul Biya to do what was politically correct by leaning toward the power bloc restructuring itself under the leadership of the USA for global economic hegemony. USA led the camp of the Western capitalists during the cold war and here was Paul Biya leaning towards the USA. To understand this move, we must regard Paul Biya as product of the pro-capitalist Roman Catholic Church that constituted a rival social category to the national liberation movement in Cameroon. . This church also stood as a rival to the French *assimilation* policy in Black Africa in general and in Cameroon in particular. The French policy of assimilation aimed to transform black Africans into black Frenchmen. It frenchified Paul Biya. Although, when the black Africans proved a more challenging transformation project than anticipated, the replacement of a similar policy of *association,* paid off all the same in that it did produced a frenchified category of Africans from among whom emerged Paul Biya. Assimilation sought to completely absorb the colonial subjects (Konde 1998: 49)...[association] sought the formation of an educated native elite who would become assimilated but who, as the leaders of the people, would remain within the framework of native society and could form an intermediary bloc between the Europeans and the native mass. In other words, association sought to make colonial subjects to see themselves as part of the greater France but not absorbed into the French political structure. As a product of the French policy of association, Paul Biya could have been no different from Ahmadou Ahidjo. It is therefore not surprising that he was going to lean towards any direction that France was leaning especially towards the end of the Cold War when new power blocs were crystallising in the world requiring those whose economies depended on international financial institutions to lean towards the side of the money. Under such an atmosphere in which the structure of international politics was changing, Paul Biya had to echo the New deal political slogan of former US president Franklin D Roosevelt in order to look legitimate in the new structure of international politics that was emerging in the world towards the end of the Cold War. In so doing, he set the stage for international capital to take over the economic base of Cameroon. When the Breton woods international financial institutions imposed harsh conditionalities on Cameroon, the response mechanism were not in place that might have successfully rescued the Cameroonian economy and turned it around as had been the case in Ghana. .

Paul Biya's New Deal effort was reflected in his speeches between 1982 and 1990. In all the speeches during this period, he stressed commitment to transforming the institutions to enable them to be more available at the service of man through the process of democratisation which, according to him, could be achieved only within a global interdependent humanity (Biya 1986: 17). His concept of a global interdependent humanity in this context meant that his New Deal sought to build an economy dependent on money derived from the aspirations of the global imperial order. This is probably so because it contradicted his idea of building an economy wherein people have greater opportunities to exercise their right to self-determination (Paul Biya 1986: 18). Building an economy that was dependent on a global interdependent humanity was soon to reveal that in the prevailing capitalist-world system where money is the king, it was those that play the drums that dictate the mode of dancing, a practice which has actually hindered the exercise of self-determination in non-European societies. While acknowledging the absence of a real nation in Cameroon due to ethnic, religious and linguistic particularities (Biya 1986: 28), he weaved a new element unto Ahmadou Ahidjo's concept of unity, namely national integration. According to the New Deal herald, national integration was the crucial stage to national unity. He modified Ahmadou Ahidjo's concept of planned liberalism into that of communal or democratic liberalism.

Although Paul Biya's political philosophy is generally full of the promises to instil a sense of belonging and that of national consciousness in all Cameroonians as well as promises to put the country's material resources at the disposal of citizens, its central tendency is towards attracting foreign capital. What looked like a social project according to Mono Ndzana (1985), in practice was not. Its central tendency is aimed at building an economy that depends on international capital. To make it look like a social project, he weaves in the idea of building an economy that is able to respond to the priorities of the citizens within a system of social justice but within the framework of an interdependent humanity as a strategy that "will enable a greater number of Cameroonians to do business without appealing to foreign capital" (Biya 1986: 63).With that in mind, he puts himself on the same pedestal like his predecessor as a crusader for international capital. Yet earlier on in his inaugural address on November 6, 1982 he acknowledged that he was taking over office at the time when Africa was engaged in the irreversible fight against what he said was the last bastion of colonialists.

Speaking at the closure of the second extraordinary congress of the CNU political party on September 14, 1983, ten months after his ascension to the supreme magistracy of the state, President Paul Biya revealed that he had perceived nation-building to be a joint enterprise between local and foreign partners just like his predecessor, Ahmadou Ahidjo. Based on his perception of nation-building as a joint partnership between citizens and foreign partners, Paul Biya said;

> "On several occasions after my accession to the highest office of the State, I have exhorted my fellow-countrymen and our various foreign partners to work hard and confidently in order to make their contributions that are irreplaceable, on the one hand, and highly appreciated on the other, to the development of the nation".

Based on this view of nation-building, Paul Biya's political, economic and social programme, became the basis of his political philosophy embodied in *Communal Liberalism* He asserted in Biya (1986: 13) that it was derived from the knowledge of our country through careful observation. It became ineluctability linked to his perception of nation-building as a partnership between foreign and local elite aimed towards achieving a more interdependent humanity, but with no intention to put in place a response mechanism that can forcefully rescue the Cameroonian economy from harsh conditionalities imposed on it by international financial agencies and turn the economy around towards achieving an economic miracle for Cameroon. A close observation of the New Deal political philosophy reveals that it seems locked up between the courting of foreign capital and the preservation of economic independence as expressed in Biya (1986: 22). Though perceiving nation-building to be a joint enterprise between local and foreign partners President Paul Biya still held that there was a need to ensure the autonomy of weak nations, among which was Cameroon, in a principle of peaceful coexistence (Biya 1986: 19).

At the Bamenda New Deal Congress of March 21-24, 1985 Paul Biya hinted that liberalisation was going to be the corner stone in his nation-building project, a process that would lead the country to the New Deal, stressing that:

> "Our present and future action will be centred around rigour in management, moralisation of behaviour, liberalisation and democratisation of public life and self-reliant and self-sustaining economic, social and cultural development which is accelerated and improved under a new style and a new dynamism."

Having defined the major guidelines of the New Deal political philosophy which included his new style and new dynamism during the Second Congress of the CNU party on October 14, 1983, he introduction into the Cameroon political lexicology the concept of democratic or communal liberalism(Biya, 1986: 30, 58). Expatriating on this new concept of democratic or communal liberalism, he explained that this concept disengages the state from its traditional role of planning and social provisioning as was the case under President Ahmadou Ahidjo. The application of this concept of democratic or communal liberalism led to a new form of direct reinvasion by multi-national corporations that had developed under the leadership of the USA. Based on the available facts, we conclude President Paul Biya, as Ntumazah (2001) maintains, was just a replay of President Ahmadou Ahidjo. The latter represented the exclusive interest of France in Cameroon. The former liberalised both the political and the economic spheres, in his attempt to create an interdependent humanity in which the country advertently falls directly under the control and devastation of multinationals as designed by the USA-based Breton Woods twins, which had imposed the structural adjustment measures on his government. Unfortunately, his political concept of communal liberalism, which was intended to put the economy at the service of the citizens of his country (Biya 1986: 75) rather liberalised communal ties and placed the economy beyond the control of Cameroonians. To tell you the truth, democratic or communal liberalism officially handed the country's economy directly to multinationals that swarmed the economy after the structure of the economy was liberalised in a process that actually gave multinationals the upper edge to economically devastate Cameroonians in their own country in the name of the World bank and the IMF, all UN specialised agencies.

Although no country is expected to be cut off from the rest of the world like a monad, Paul Biya's New Deal political philosophy, which laid stress on a more interdependent humanity is misleading. Interdependent humanity is achieved not by presidential decrees. Interdependent humanity is the political talk of a politician using approximate language to buy time. To buy time, politicians fill the air with fleeting illusions and want the people to take fleeting illusions for fact. To mull over this point, let us examine one example.

The Euphoric Fad of the New Deal Herald

On the back cover of her book Marie-Louise Eteki-Otabela (1987) poses a question of national interest as to whether the resigning of President Ahmadou Ahidjo as President of Cameroon implied the end of totalitarianism in Cameroon and the installation of a new system of government based on a new vision of society or not. The literature reveals that, but for the enactment of the liberal laws on free expression and association in 1990, the passage from President Ahmadou Ahidjo to President Paul Biya was an inheritance in that the class structure that subjects 85 Percent of Cameroonians was maintained (Nyamnjoh 1999: 105; Ngayap 1983: 105; Eteki Otabela 1989: 21). President Paul Biya simply acted as a new executor of the same agendas designed by European countries (Woungly-Massaga 1984: 117; Ntumazah 2001). To carry on with the further verification of our hypothesis as to whether the New Deal political philosophy was a neo-ahidjoism or not, we address this: Was the New Deal political philosophy conceived with a clear intention in mind to apply a forceful strategy that would turn the economy around to achieve an economic marvel for the economy to bear fruits that will trickle down to the grassroots or was it just a fleeting illusion emanating from the thinking mind of a politician who just wanted to look legitimate in the eyes of voters?

Paul Biya's accession to the presidency, though unplanned, came with some euphoria. To Cameroonians emerging from a system of tyranny, it was like bidding farewell to a nightmare. Paul Biya was something of an enigma. Eventually, the period between 1982, when he came to power and 1987 when SAP went operational, Cameroonians expected much from him (Charly Gabriel Mbock 1985: 121; Eteki-Otabela 1987: 80). Even after SAP was implemented Cameroonians were still revelling, whooping it up, and could not quickly adjust their mind-set to come to terms with the brutal reality as planned for him by the Western countries through the Breton Woods twin multilateral corporations, the IMF/World Bank, all UN specialised agencies. The distraction was total and the 1984 attempted coup d'état provided more than just a distraction. It drew sympathy to the new President (Ngayap 1983; Henri Bandolo 1985: 279). And so when the IMF/World Bank draconian policy prescriptions some Cameroonian who ardently supported the new era, an era incarnated by the elegant new president who came preaching rigour and moralisation, dismissed the news as mere rumour (Eleih-Elle 1993: 39).

Eleih-Elle Etian recalls that President Paul Biya was himself surprised to become the new head of state. Like everyone, Etian holds that initially Paul Biya had no vision for any type of society. He had had no time to reflect on a political programme for such a project when constitutionally appointed (Eleih-Elle 1993: 1-4). With no vision for society he, therefore, had no counterpoising legislation against foreign influences. Like his predecessor Biya placed himself at the disposal of France who designed for him programmes under the heading of planned liberalism. President Paul Biya also pledged to continue with the programme of planned liberalism (Woungly-Massaga 1984: 116). He thus placed himself at the service of the World Bank/IMF who imposed the political/economic programme of liberalisation and privatisation on him, the implementation of which left a trail of disastrous social, economic, cultural, environmental, and political consequences on Cameroon following the assault by multi-nationals on the liberalised terrain in Cameroon. Consequently, Paul Biya, like his predecessor, was forced to abandon his decision to continue with planed Liberalism. It was at this point that Paul Biya decided to elaborate what became the New Deal political philosophy for society in *Communal Liberation* (1986). Under the overwhelming influences of external forces, President Paul Biya was compelled to abandon planned liberalism in exactly the same way President Ahmadou Ahidjo was compelled to abandon his political ideas of African Socialism. In response to the externally imposed political thinking engineered by the Bretton Woods institutions, *Communal Liberation* served as a distraction, and opened the country's economy to be reclaimed by multinationals as illustrated in table 1 below.

Nevertheless, according to Mono Ndzana (1985) Paul Biya's political philosophy bore a semblance of a social agenda. Eleih-Elle (1993), observes that Cameroon's political chapter under President Paul Biya, which opened with a series of calamities, ranging from catastrophic accidents to natural disasters, to the April 1984 coup d'état, to the economic crisis, might have contributed one way or another to alter President Paul Biya's approach to nation-building. Going even further, Eleih-Elle describes President Biya as a man of classical culture with moral probity who, according to him, was the rightful person to rescue Cameroon's economy from extravertism and the fight for personal enrichment that characterised the Ahidjo regime (Eleih-Elle1993: 7-22). According to Eleih-Elle, President Paul Biya's economic therapy for the economic crisis, being that of austerity measures, which included the withdrawal of public spending on social provisioning (P.139), was the most appropriate for Cameroon.

With these measures, he goes on to say, the state under Paul Biya's 10 years in office (in 1993) was able to achieve much in terms of infrastructure more than under Ahidjo (P.158). At the socio-cultural level Eleih-Elle (1993: 157-171) assesses President Paul Biya's idea for Cameroon in the domain of solarisation, sports, and music as having been characterised by momentous achievements. Politically, he presents President Paul Biya as having achieved much for Cameroon in terms of stability, peace and order that reigns in the country in spite of internal agitations (Eleih-Elle Ibid: 171). In an assessment of the first twelve years of President Paul Biya, a group of authors in *Le Renouveau Cameroun* (1983), points out that Paul Biya's vision for Cameroon is that of establishing an economy that combines with political liberalism aimed at gaining the interest of foreign donors (P.186). The strategy to achieving this, they maintained, was by liberalising the institutions and to open debates (P.215), as a process in democratisation (P. 217), through social justice (P.260).

In spite of this rosy picture of President Biya's term of office, the critical section of literature holds a contrary opinion. These critics argues that the application of President Paul Biya's political idea rather turned Cameroon into the most corrupt country in the world, according to a criteria adopted by Transparency International. In line with this contrary opinion,

Nyamnjoh (1999) contends that President Biya's presidency was marked by

".... the politics of regional and ethnic balance, the chronic lack of vision as a country, the lack of real commitment to democracy, the propensity to vacillate on most issues of collective interest, together with an infinite inability to pursue common interests and aspirations. All that appears to unite Cameroonians is a common ethnic or regional ambition to preserve differences under the delusion of maximising opportunities" (Nyamnjoh 1999: 101).

The difference between President Paul Biya and President Ahmadou Ahidjo seems to be in the different epochs in which they operated. The economic exigencies of European countries marked the different epochs of the two presidents Ahidjo operated during the period in which imperial states subjugated and exploited indirectly through neo-colonial states after a semblance of independence was granted. , Biya operated in an era when European multi-national corporations invaded in the name of the major international organisations such as the UN through the IMF and World Bank that imposed the conditionalities on Paul Biya. These conditions produced the desired effects for multinationals that represented Western interests.

Austerity measures that constituted President Paul Biya's economic therapy included liberalisation and privatisation, imposed on Cameroon by the World Bank/IMF, all UN specialised agencies as part of the Structural Adjustment Plan (SAP) that went operational on July 1, 1987. Without making any allusion to its external imposition, SAP was actually announced by President Paul Biya himself in parliament on June 20th 1987. Implementation of SAP spelled disaster and misery for Cameroonians, especially following the stoppage of employment within the public service, the trimming of the overstaffed public service[1], the privatisation of government run para-statals, salary cuts, and the devaluation of the FCFA by 50%.

Between 1987 and 1994, 20.000 civil servants lost their jobs, 40.000 workers in the industrial sector were laid off representing 12 % employment in the non-agricultural sector (Kengne Fodouop 1997: 150). Coupled with a 70 % salary cut of 1993, and the January 1994 devaluation of the FCFA by 50 %, the standards of living of the Cameroonian family declined precipitously (Aloysius Ajab Amin 1997: 58). The forceful reintroduction of multi-party politics in 1990 and the October 1992 Presidential elections ended in controversy with the opposition political parties' call for "Ghost Towns". This unrest further crippled the already ailing economy and exacerbated ethnic tensions that had previously been held in check under Ahmadou Ahidjo by military force.

President Biya's tenure of office was thus characterised by unemployment and poverty, dashing the hopes of Cameroonians who had hailed his vision for society as preached by him, outlined in *Communal Liberalism* (1986), as messianic. The plight of Cameroonians was further accentuated by Paul Biya's *laissez allez* attitude, not only in his failure to punish the ethno-political barons of his regime for stealing public money[2], but his opening up of the economy to multiple multi-nationals. This has led to a situation where almost all sectors of the economy are facing an unfair competition from a foreign entrepreneurial category[3]. His government's inability to appropriately reallocate the resources of the nation in a way to achieve national integration and sustained economic growth (Fondo Sikod 1997) has not only exasperated the crisis that epitomises the collapse

---

[1] The Biya regime increased the number of civil servants from 80.000 in 1982 to about 180.000 in 1988 most of who were from his Beti ethnic group (see Konings and Nyamnjoh 2003).

[2] President Biya is on record for asking for proofs to punish culprits.

[3] Even privatisation has come to mean the selling of what Cameroonians consider to be their national patrimony to foreign companies

of the economy, but has also led to internal political and social discord in the process of ethno-political competition for a share of what is perceived to be a national cake.

In announcing the coming of SAP in parliament on June 20th 1987, Paul Biya told Cameroonians that the structural adjustment measures the World Bank and IMF had imposed on Cameroon that very year as conditionalities for loans to Cameroon, would render the Public Service more efficient and state corporations more productive. On the contrary, the public service has become highly corrupt and inefficient while the corporations that were sold out very cheaply to multi-nationals did not improve in terms of output. On the whole, privatisation turned out to be an economic disaster for Cameroon and Cameroonians

Table 1: Effects of SAP on Cameroon's "Economy"

No	States Corporations Closed	Banks Closed	State Corporations Privatised
1	National Produce Marketing Board	Cameroon Bank	SONEL
2	SODECAO	Crédit Agricole	CDC- Tea Estates
3	Benoue Development Authority	BIAO-Meridien	CDC-Banana Estates
4	FONADER	-	REGIFERCAM
5	ZAPI-EST	-	BICIC
6	National Research Projects	-	HEVECAM
7	CELLUCAM	-	SOCAPALM
8	SODERIM	-	CAMTEL
9	WADA	-	SOCAR
10	AMACAM	-	SNEC
11	CNR	-	CAMSUCO
12	SOTUC	-	CamPost
13	MIDEVIV	-	SCB
14	WESTCORN	-	-
15	SODEBLE	-	-
16	MISSAMBE	-	-
17	CAMAIR	-	-

Under the liberalisation agendas of the late 1980s, which spanned into the 1990s, privatisation in Cameroon spelled disaster for Cameroonians. The whole exercise turned out to achieve the exact opposite of what Cameroonians had expected. A few examples will elucidate the point. The National Electricity Corporation (SONEL)[4] that became AES SONEL after it was sold to an American company, AES sirocco, did not show any real improvement in terms of productivity. Immediately after privatization, the firm plunged the country into more frequent and protracted power cuts than Cameroonians had known before. Such a disaster probably alleged proof that the Americans inherited a corporation in a very bad state thus justifying why it had to be sold to "those who can better manage it". The long and unpredictable power cuts affected the economy adversely, bringing it to further ruin. The privatisation of the National Railway Corporation (RNCF) to a French company instead saw the Nkongsamba link cut off, while the French owners of the corporation preferred to use the old and dilapidated trains and the colonial infrastructure for the transportation of goods only since that was seen to be more profitable. When the tea sector of the Cameroon Development Corporation (CDC) was sold to a South African company in 2002, over 1000 workers were immediately retrenched, and those who were retained on the payroll of the corporation had their fringe benefits withdrawn with no improvement in living conditions in the camps[5]. Strikes and protestations became a frequent occurrence in the working life in that sector of the CDC immediately privatization.

To say that "Paul Biya's policy of liberalisation was to attract foreign donors" as the authors of *Le Renouveau Cameroun* (1983) put it, is to say the obvious. His duty, like that of his predecessor,

---

[4] Electricity in Cameroon was first produced by the French for use at the Alucam Company in the French territory, which became ENELCAM, and by the British for use in the CDC plantations, which became Powercam. The two ventures merged in the 1970s to become the National Electricity Corporation (SONEL).

was to obey the instructions of his metropolitan patrons, who are his associates in the development or underdevelopment of Cameroon, which is very visible in *Communal Liberalism*. The heart of the matter is that the transmigration of capital is for profit motives and thus has no social agenda. With no social agenda it has nothing to do with issues of collective interests and can only create social problems. Talk of rendering state corporations more productive only mystifies processes whereby national patrimony is sold to foreign companies.

The New Deal Political Programme

Apparently originating his political philosophy from the same brain wave as Ahmadou Ahidjo, President Paul Biya's New Deal political programme seems to reflect that of his predecessor in which the nation-building project is all about the craving for foreign partners. According to Paul Biya's New Deal political programme, the state must be a business enterprise with foreign partners as major actors. Even his foreign policy seems to reflect this brain wave too since it is derived from the central idea of his political philosophy, which was, like that of Ahmadou Ahidjo before him, to bring about a more interdependent mankind. Inadvertently, Paul Biya's New Deal political programme is tailored to achieve the globalisation agenda as driven by multi-nationals and donor agencies. Although it overtly claims that it is intended essentially "to serve the foremost interest of our people [Cameroonians] in an increasingly interdependent world" (Biya 1986: 17), it essentially positions the lives of Cameroonians on a path of exploitation by multi-nationals. The programme's recognition of the craving by powerful nations to dominate and exploit the weaker ones, and also the need for states to be independent and free from imperial domination within such an imbalanced world order was mitigated by the unwillingness of its designer to break relations with foreign economic partners (Biya 1986: 66). While the disinclination to break relations with foreign economic partners and achieving freedom from imperial domination is similar to that of Ahmadou Ahidjo in intent it is different from that of Ahmadou Ahidjo only in that, while Ahmadou Ahidjo sought to subject Cameroonians under the yoke of imperial domination by achieving unity by the whip, Paul Biya sought to subject Cameroonians under the yoke of imperial domination by liberalising communalities., By freeing the political sphere to enable his foreign partners/multi-nationals to regain the economy especially at a time when communism in the Soviet Union had been dismantled there was no longer a need for "dictatorship" in Africa. After the fall of communism there was no need for a dictatorial president in Africa who needed to "bully" Africans away from a "frightful" communism. This opportunity to shift to a new form of economic hegemony was particularly facile in the case of African countries which no longer languished under the static monopoly control of only one European country.

Recognising bilingualism as an added advantage for Cameroon, the New Deal political programme is tailored on the virtues of bilingualism as a political instrument for projecting Cameroon's cultural identity intended "to open up our country to the great civilisation of today" (Biya 1986: 34). Coupled with its craze for foreign partners, bilingualism is used as a best-seller to attract foreign partners especially as linguistically speaking, Cameroon falls directly under foreign control, rendering the craving for national independence an impossible task. As a matter of fact, Paul Biya's New Deal political agenda puts the New Deal political philosopher on the straight path with his predecessor, Ahmadou Ahidjo. *Communal Liberalism,* is essentially a political philosophy with multidimensional implications, intended to restore the autonomy of Man in the various areas of the social, economic, intellectual, political and religious life (Biya 1986: 114). When examined closely it reveals its post-colonial predispositions in which Africans are not their own subjects but are rather objects of the subjecting subject, subjected to the exigencies of global imperial order. This is actually the kind of predilection that sets in motion the post-colonial era in Africa in general in which the economic life of the state is almost wholly in the hands of foreign business concerns. In effect, the political programme of the communal liberal philosopher, Paul Biya, hands the economic life of the state to foreign business concerns, probably through privatisation as Cameroonians saw it happened. Paul Biya's New Deal political programme or agenda is one that depersonalises political power while still leaving the handle of political power in the hands of the president.

> "From the political stand point, this philosophy is concerned with the depersonalisation of political power as opposed to the feudal system which is based on more or less legal personal relations which lead to confusion between the political authority and the individual's inalienable rights" (Biya 1986: 113).

As such, the New Deal political philosopher does not seem to harbour the intention to develop a political philosophy that empowers the individual to act freely to change his/her condition of dehumanisation under the post-colonial power structure. Rather, he tacitly returns to the Cartesian concept of the individual. This is possible because Cameroon as a state lacks a solid ideological base that constitutes the moral-rational basis for the horizontal relationship between its people, the vertical relations within the power structure, and the relationship between its people and the physical world for human well-being, based on which the process for the systematic growth of spheres for the management of public affairs should derive its legitimisation., President Paul Biya's political programme was intended to transform the political institutions with the view to establishing a new political society for human well-being, with the expected results being the depersonalisation of political power. This programme was pegged on three cardinal principles; achieving national unity, democratisation; and globalisation

(Biya 1986: 27). Some of the major pre-occupations of the New Deal are the desire to bequeath to history a solid nation-state, which is constituted of two components; the state which is an instrument for the organisation of political power, and a nation, which provides the framework of human solidarity. Moreover, his concept of depersonalising state power failed to solve the problem of corruption which, in the case of Cameroon, can be seen as the by-product of the racket system that is tangled up with a foreign category on which Cameroon was founded and on which it thrives.

While a strong state was going to control the instruments of coercion such as the army, police, and the prison, aimed at instilling order (Biya 1986: 28, 47), the "nation-state", for its part was to be…

> "… characterised by a partial or total combination of certain specific material and spiritual elements which reinforce its homogeneity and its member's awareness of unity… a union of communities with one race, language, territory, economic life and history" (Biya 1986: 29).

Such a definition of a nation takes into account the fact that a linking element is required to attain internal unity. This fact would indicate that, at least President Paul Biya was aware that nation-building is much more than just the manipulation of human and economic forces by the use of the coercive instruments of the state under legislation for the growth and expansion of the global imperial order. Better still more than for the thriving of the global imperial order acting through multi-nationals. Like his predecessor he opted for the unrealistic approach of wishing away the ethnic factor by calling on citizens to consider themselves first of all Cameroonians before Bamileke, Ewondo, Foulbe, Bassa, Boulou, Douala, Bakweri, Baya, Massa, or Maka (see his speech of September 14, 1983). But a nation is not built by wishing away its roots as Paul Biya (1986) like Ahidjo upholds. A nation is built by the people themselves galvanising their actions and acting through social engagements to achieving well defined objectives vital for their existence. By asking people to abandon their identities in exchange of promises is an unrealistic political gimmick. The whole nation cannot depend on the wishes of an individual if such an individual is not representing something other than the real concern of the people.

Under Ahmadou Ahidjo a call was made for ethno-political entities to abandon the rational basis of communal belonging for dependence on the state structure. Under Paul Biya, the same call, in the spirit of communal liberalism, completely dislocated the rational basis of social bonds in readiness for the new economic assault on the people by the US-based Britton Woods institutions. Otherwise, by abandoning the ethno-political identities as indigenous people were being called upon to do, what were they expected to become? French? English? Cameroonians? If the intention is for them to become Cameroonians, what is the cultural identity of Cameroon that matches that of the Douala, the Bamileke, the Kom, the Nso, etc., as Mveng (1985) had attempted to question.

Thus, attempts "to inculcate in every Cameroonian a deep-seated national awareness which cannot be shaken by a primary and instinctive attachment to tribal and regional values and interests" (Biya 1986: 30– 31) ought to have been rooted on the ethno-political particularities and interests that are evident and constitutes the basis of ethno-regional politics in Cameroon which Nyamnjoh (1999) points out. This ethno-regional politics, which was further exacerbated by the fact that political power in Cameroon under Paul Biya, like his predecessor, was never really separated, constituting a breeding ground for social ills such as tribalism, corruption, favouritism, etc., is characteristic of political life in Cameroon. Established as a racket system by European profiteers in their mission to steal natural resources and to enslave local people for the advancement of European interests, thrives on the basis of these social ills.

However, to get to his envisaged new political society that would supposedly meet the needs of all Cameroonians (Biya 1986: 12), Paul Biya promised new dynamism that would improve on the political institutions to achieve a true and authentic democracy within an open society. The New Deal political concept of an open society means that citizens could act freely, combining experience and hope for the future to satisfy their basic needs in order and liberty aimed at achieving progress and equilibrium. He contends that unity will combine diversity in a complementary manner to achieve political solidarity for people of diverse backgrounds bound together for a common geographical, historical, linguistic, tribal and religious destiny typical of a modern state. This implied the adoption of a European-style secular state over which reigns the President, independent of his religious orientation and ethnic background, impartial in the discharge of his duty to the nation. In other words, national unity implied waging a war against tribalism, all sorts of favouritism, and all systems of sectarian privileges to encourage the spirit of national consciousness (Biya 1986: 27).

Before the representatives of the global imperial order imposed their valets on Africans to assist in their mission of global domination, ethno-political entities existed with their particularisms. These particularisms did not exclude universalisms amongst them. European invaders and their valets imposed a power structure on the people without their consent based on no social contract. This contract defined for the parties from the very onset the gains and the sacrifices such a venture entails. The processes that led to the emergence of an entity called Cameroon occurred in an unplanned manner. Cameroonians suddenly learned that they have a prime minister who evolved into a president and who unleashed terror on them within a power structure that had very drastically curtailed their autonomy and freedom. Suddenly still, in 1982, a new president was again enthroned in almost the same way as the first. During these transitions, from the reign of terror to liberalism of which they had no say, only the ethno-political entity was a sure source of social security for the citizens who had become subjects - not citizens - under the post-colonial state. On what basis, therefore, were Cameroonians expected to abandon their ethno-political particularisms as Paul Biya, like his predecessor, proposed? Or better still, why were they expected to abandon their attachments to communities that were built on concrete reality, which still met their hopes and aspirations, to one that built on a day dream, imposed on them by foreigners? A modern state that is static in character as what one finds in Cameroon cannot replace a nation that emerges from the rational will of the people who have decided to organise themselves into a larger entity. Paul Biya like Ahidjo before him failed to imagine such a nation and so failed to come up with a political programme to nourish the home-grown foundation of the nation from within. Now that we have thoroughly examined Paul Biya's New Deal political programme, we turn to the New Deal economic programme.

The New Deal Economic Programme

President Paul Biya's economic model of communal liberalism as outlined in his book *Communal Liberalism* ineluctably links up to his political philosophy. The resulting construct creates a political/economic model that upholds the role of the state as business enterprise. The purpose of this shift from state as contract with the governed to state as business is to partner with any foreign entity at the expense of the wellbeing and enfranchisement of the Cameroonian people. In outlining his economic programme in communal liberalism, Paul Biya states that his economic programme for Cameroon is based on an economic model "characterised by free enterprise and a concern for national solidarity which behoves of a strong state to impress upon all its economic partners through appropriate regulation" (Biya 1986:57). Hence, it reflected his post-colonial prejudices in which democracy is conceived as a buzz word. Conceived as a buzz word in the post-colonial context, democracy only helps to open up the political sphere for the foreign economic partners of the business state to thrive in business while citizens are only the subordinated category in a dependent economic system that subjugates them. This, seems to be the meaning beneath the philosophy of liberalism. Liberalism grounded in the Western concept of liberal democracy in the context of Cameroon was not guarantee of active citizen involvement in decision-making. Rather in Cameroon liberalism legitimised the triumph of big business concerns acting on the terms of international financial agencies, serving as major actors. This economic hegemony came at a time when citizens were economically gagged by the tyrannical state under Ahmadou Ahidjo, at a time corresponding to the dismantling of the Soviet Union and much of communism. The Cold War was coming to an end. There was no need in the West for the tyrannical state in Africa. In tune with the spirit of the Washington Consensus, communal liberalism thus rooted itself in the desire to open up Cameroon for corporate business from diverse origins in a context where disadvantaged citizens struggled to compete with foreign business on their own soil. That is the historical context that gave birth to communal liberalism. To better respond to the demands of the Washington consensus, communal liberalism was veiled in the principles of:

- Democratic planning;
- Priority to agriculture;
- Assistance to small and medium-sized undertakings and the development of heavy equipment;
- Mastery of science and technology;
- Greater efficiency of our services;
- National economic independence (Biya: ibid)
-

In spite of what looks like a philosophy for national economic independence, Paul Biya's post-colonial economic programme the philosophers' design imagines that foreign partners and foreign capital was going to play a dominant role in of this economic programme. According to the tenets of the New Deal economic programme, citizens should play a "participatory" role only in exactly the same way as it was obliquely stated in the Gaullist doctrine of "participation". In Gaullist doctrine "participation" meant foreigners were the major economic actors and citizens were to merely participate, minimally in the economic life of their own country. Application of Gaullist doctrine of "participation" resulted in the economic disaster of the late 1980s and also fuelled wide spread corruption that radiated throughout the rungs of society from top down. Then again, communal liberalism envisioned agricultural production increases by organising villages into autonomous communities for large-scale agricultural production and enterprises. Attention paid to food crop farmers provided loans from financial houses and farm implements dealers (Biya 1986: 61). Communal liberalism equally envisioned that mastery of science constituted the basis for development of heavy industries including agricultural and food processing industries (Biya 1986: 63, 64) as necessary steps in achieving economic independence. However, in practice, that was not what Cameroonians saw happen. For example, the disappearance under SAP of the structures to ensure sustainability thwarted the New Deal economic plan to give priority to agriculture. Thus productivity in the agricultural production chain instead slowed. The disappearance under SAP of structures such as ONCPB for example, that sustained productivity actually whirled unprecedented problems relating to output in the agricultural sector instead. Under the overwhelming pressure put on him by the initiators of SAP there was just no way the New Deal political philosopher could have insisted on giving priority to agriculture as he had thought.

With respect to freeing the economy from foreign influences, Paul Biya, like Ahmadou Ahidjo before him who had used almost these same words in describing his economic programme for Cameroon, contends that it would be absurd to think of an economic system that does not have an exchange with the outside world (Biya 1986: 66). As true as this assertion may be, it is not the same thing as having an economy that relies heavily on foreign capital for financing because even he himself acknowledged that;

> "We cannot say a country is independent as long as its citizens continue to seek foreign capital to finance even the smallest development ventures" (Biya 1986: 67).

Although he knows too well that democratic planning does not mean subordinating the economy of a country to foreign interests (Biya 1986: 128), Communal Liberalism achieved that very thing for Cameroon. The application of democratic or communal liberalism only succeeded in subordinating the country to the interests of the international financial institutions. This subordination outshined the ability of Cameroonians to realise projects by themselves for themselves using their own means. His concept of Cameroon developing as a monad or as an autarchy (Biya 1986: 66), a view shared by his predecessor, was misplaced. At no time in the history of Africa has any society ever been an autarchy. On the contrary, pre-modern African societies were relatively autonomous yet interdependent; sharing items on all aspects of life on equal terms (see for example Warnier 1975; 1983). Warnier just quoted identifies a purely indigenous concept of interdependent humanity which was halted with the advent of the nation-state when arbitrary boundaries were imposed on indigenous peoples by fraudulent European invaders.

Prior to the invasion of Africa by the fraudulent Europeans a system of agriculture was practiced whereby almost everybody was a farmer growing a variety of food crops which were consumed and redistributed across the borders within an economic system that spanned the length and breadth of Africa. This constituted the main economic chain that linked vast populations together across Africa. In pre-modern times in Africa, ecological sustainability was ensured by a system of shifting agriculture which ensured long fallow periods since farmers had free access to land. As early as the 1930s, especially with the advent of colonisation when export crops such as cacao, coffee, banana and rubber were introduced, and were grown in plantations on large scale using external inputs for external markets, there was the tendency for local people to abandon agricultural activities in favour of export crops. Export crops thus became the major focus of Cameroon's macro economy and research. In 1972, when President Ahmadou Ahidjo launched the famous Green Revolution in Buea, a system of mono-cropping and the use of chemical inputs was encouraged with government giving credits to farmers and subsidising up to 65% and 100% of the cost of fertilizer and pesticides, respectively. Consequently, many farmers shifted toward producing export crops and became heavily dependent on external markets and farm inputs from government.

During President Paul Biya's first decade in office and coeval to the publication of his political philosophy in which he outlined his economic programme for Cameroon, the implementation of SAP, a World Bank/IMF economic prescription for Cameroon, completely sabotaged the economy in general and the agricultural sector in particular when some major para-statals were sold off to foreign companies in the spirit of communal liberalism and many others were closed down. During his second decade in office, a series of devastating features shook the nation. Among the devastating features that shook the nation were, the devaluation of the FCFA by 50 %, a 70 % salary slash for the public sector workers, the withdrawal of subsidies and farm inputs, the discrediting of the customary land tenure which granted land use rights to women and the eventual imposition of a land tenure law $N^0 74/1$ of July 6, 1974. This law was inherited from the colonial system in which the state hijacked all lands, used or unused, except corporate lands on which there were still large agro-industrial plantations serving foreign economic interests. For its part, this land tenure law limited the space for citizen's involvement in food production on a scale that can even feed a family throughout the year. The imposition of this post-colonial land tenure law actually mitigated attempts by local farmers to fall back on food crop cultivation. Unfortunately this imposition took place at a period when a rapid urbanisation rate had clustered an unproductive population in "towns" which sprawled onto arable lands which otherwise would have been useful for agricultural production.

Even efforts by local farmers; the rural dwellers who were still disposed to arable lands, to regain their sector were frustrated by the fact that government's liberal laws (liberalism) favoured the importation of food stuffs and dairy products which flooded the local markets at very cheap prices and completely damaged local food production. It was possible to buy foreign rice or imported dyoxinated chicken, for example, in a local market at a cost lower than the cost of producing it in Cameroon. This economic practice not only forced farmers to abandon farming but also forced Cameroonians to become increasingly dependent on imported food to the disadvantage of local food production, thus hampering food security needs in spite of Paul Biya's economic programme intended to give "priority to agriculture". An economic programme that merely expresses the intention to "give priority to agriculture" instead gave priority to foreign business which completely overran the economy and rendered Cameroonians an economically marginal people on their own soil (see table 1 above).

The New Deal Social Programme

From the look of things, one may be tempted to conclude that President Paul Biya did not have any social programme given that all what was put in place under President Ahmadou Ahidjo was dismantled since the cold war was over and there was nothing for the white race to worry about anymore, leaving Paul Biya only with the floating of slogans for the fight against this and the fight against that. But according to President Paul Biya, he had envisioned a programme for the social transformation of Cameroonians which was to culminate in producing citizens who are fully aware of their rights and responsibilities as citizens and to provide them with the possibilities of assuming and playing their role as citizens. This, according to him was to be achieved through the Western system of education and the Western health system, which unfortunately, constituted integral facets of the European political philosophy of invasion, control, domination, and destruction.

In the domain of education, just like Ahmadou Ahidjo before him had envisioned, it was to be made more available. All towns and hinterlands would have schools so that all Cameroonian children should have access to education in conformity with the principle of social justice and equilibrium, and for ensuring mass education. In the domain of health, President Biya envisioned a holistic health system for Cameroon that takes care of the "physical, mental, and moral health" (Biya 1986: 76) of its citizens as a true social security system. He recognised the fact that the other congenial aspects of the political life would be impossible to achieve unless health was given top priority. However, the question can be asked as to how equity was going to be achieved in a way that those in the enslaved hinterlands were going to enjoy the same health amenities as those in the major conurbations of Yaoundé and Douala where most of the country's development infrastructure are based. In his dream to restore social justice, he imagined a housing scheme, though not massive, but satisfactory to a considerable degree. For "it would be demagogic and utopian to promise to provide every Cameroonian with free housing or with a home of his choice" (Biya ibid: 77). The idea was to free housing from availability only to the privileged class to include farmers in the rural areas through a loan scheme. His vision of social equality, equity and equilibrium as strategies of achieving equality among the citizenry, was contradicted by saying;

"Since the building of our country is inevitably a collective task, an enormous task to which each citizen makes a contribution according to his means and abilities, it would be injustice of the highest order to institutionalise inequalities between effort and remuneration among workers. Such injustice existed and is still widespread in our society, leading to a great deal of frustration, complexes and eventually resignations. That is why we opted to raise the lowest salaries and wages substantially" (Biya ibid: 78).

In spite of this piece of beautiful literature, facts on the ground show that Cameroonians experienced the lowest salaries under the reign of President Paul Biya. Be that as it may, embodied in the New Deal social programme was an assurance for his country men and women. According to the New Deal social programme, Paul Biya's regime was going to put in place a system governed purely by merit. Promotion would be based purely on merit and everybody would occupy only the post that he or she deserved without regard to ethnic background or social relationship. However the record shows that meritocracy was thrown to the dogs under the New deal social programme. Within six years of President Biya's reign in Cameroon, the public service was overstaffed and the number of civil servants was more than doubled from 80.000 in 1982 to about 180.000 in 1988 with most of the irregularly recruited civil servants coming from the same Beti ethnic group as the President (see Konings and Nyamnjoh 2003). Yet still, on paper, he had a system in which there would be the equal distribution of the fruits of growth through in an effort to "eliminate all sorts of difference which contradict the principle of equality" (Biya ibid). Although, Paul Biya (1986: 114) treats law as being the symbol of impersonal power, which is a *sine qua non* for Man to enjoy his liberties, he does this as though law was a neutral or an impartial phenomenon. The application of law in Cameroon has never been neutral or impartial. The law was meant to protect foreign systems in Cameroon and those in high offices (Joseph 1978;

Abel Eyinga 1978; Mongo Beti 1984). It was destined to protect a certain category of people against the other. In reality, therefore, this ideal of social justice became a near impossibility to achieve in practice since Paul Biya spent his time in office implementing World Bank/IMF imposed programmes in Cameroon; programmes which have nothing to do with the people and their social well-being. The law protects foreign interests in Cameroon. In practice President Paul Biya's New Deal government had no clear cut social programme. He based his social policy on the famous "fight against poverty" slogan which consisted mainly of making sporadic goodwill gestures to selected sections of the public based on their support of the ruling CPDM political party.

Liberalisation entail no social programme since privatisation, a major component of the liberalisation package, meant the sale of para-statals corporations to foreign companies for their business seeking ventures leaving citizens at the mercy of foreign business concerns. Nowhere in the world has foreign business proven to have a social responsibility. Privatisation did not mean that Cameroonians could take-over the management of those strategic sectors of the economy for their own social wellbeing. Privatization did not mean that Cameroonians could take-over the management of the energy sector for their own needs or take-over the running of the water supply system for their own consumption, etc. All in all, the concern with the liberalisation of the political domain did not permit the New Deal political philosopher to come up with a social programme that enabled the popular involvement of citizens in the governing process, through which they could work out their own social programmes for their own wellbeing. The New Deal social programme withdrew government spending on social services, reduced the salaries of public sector workers against the backdrop of a devalued FCFA, and reduced local food production. Under the New Deal social programme, all of these reduced the standards of living of Cameroonians, thereby achieving for Cameroon a social disaster just like in the economic sector where an economic disaster was also recorded. Now that we have examined the political, economic and social aspects of the New Deal Programme, for a comprehensive view of the New Deal political philosophy, we now turn to the New Deal cultural programme.

The New Deal Cultural Programme

President Paul Biya's New Deal cultural policy, like that of Ahmadou Ahidjo before him, did not really envisage the putting in place of a worthwhile cultural policy for Cameroon. An examination of the cultural policies of both men tends to show disregarded the great diversity of cultural units that exist in Cameroon and treated them from an unrealistic perspective. President Paul Biya in charting his New Deal cultural policy may have intended to create a value system based on existing cultural values (Biya 1986: 101). New Deal cultural policy aimed to produce a cultural spiritualism rooted in reality, void of idle dreams; a cultural spiritualism in which matter is controlled purely by the spirit. It failed to state the role the indigenous peoples, inventors of the indigenous cultures of Cameroon, were going to play in realising the cultural project. In the final analysis, the advent of the two successive post-colonial regimes in Cameroon failed to put in place a clear cut cultural policy. This failure could explain why cultural issues such as those relating to books, music, artworks, are being handled haphazardly. It is unimaginable that for over three decades in office, the New Deal political philosopher did not find it expedient to put in place a cultural policy that defines the status of artists and musicians or put in place a book policy that ensures the effective production, distribution and consumption of books. Consider that books have always played a key determinant role in the development process by the intellectual and literary products they foster as an integral part of the society they represent. In spite of this over sight, the cultural policy of the New Deal was to build for Cameroon an eclectic personality provided Cameroonians were not to confuse the disintegration of the existing cultures or to create a disparity or the dispersal of the ethnic cultures (Biya 1986: 102). This haphazard policy did not state the processes through which the reconstruction of a national culture from the pre-existing ones was to be achieved.

With respect to building a national language, Paul Biya was aware of the fact that language embodies the cultural processes of a people (Biya 1986: 104). He then proposed an approach in which our "cultural heritage will be translated into reality at the national level to the great benefit of the national community" (Biya 1986: 104). Unfortunately, Paul Biya's political philosophy was limited by the entrapments of the bourgeois ideas of the post-colonial era. Such entrapments misled the New Deal political philosopher into mistaking the manifest aspects of culture (Biya 1986: 106), for cultural spiritualism. Definitely yes, cultural spiritualism is the inner essence of culture out of which a national language can emerge to serve as the collective social memory of the cultural processes that has produced it.

In terms of cultural orientation and training, the New Deal cultural programme targeted the family as a strategy to groom Cameroonians in human values. The New Deal cultural programme also targeted the professional orientation of young Cameroonians to gradually shift the basis of education from mere certificate oriented to skill development so that Cameroonians could be more useful and also to include human rights. Although there was an intention to build a national culture by putting in place a system, which will gradually integrate the ethnic cultures into a national culture, this was done in a superficial manner, in complete ignorance of the cultural matrix of indigenous Cameroon. Linguistically, the process was to follow a two-stage process. While encouraging the development of the diverse ethnic language at local level, at national level, national integration was to be achieved through the promotion of the two European colonial inherited languages. Here the New Deal cultural programme focused on achieving the goal of global citizenship or what its designer referred to as a "more interdependent mankind".

Neither culture nor language is decreed into existence from behind an executive desk. As a social invention, culture emerges naturally from the daily activities of the people as they struggle to respond to the law of causality that organises their world, unobservable to them. When culture emerges through this processes, it develops into a system of interrelated meanings, expressed through such symbolic representations as sets of rules, norms, proverbs, dictums, beliefs, division of labour, etc., that guide human thought and action, upheld by the people themselves within the context of their worldview which in turn structures the language which classifies both their social and material world all of which makes social life within that context possible. The people's identity becomes and embodiment of all of that and distinguishes them from other human communities far or near; becoming an exclusive domain of reality which can be understood only from its own specificity.

The New Deal Strategy

Like former president Ahmadou Ahidjo who envisaged a strong state and a powerful president as his strategy of achieving unity by the whip which was an unarticulated requirement for the subordination of Cameroonians under his political and economic whims and that of his foreign partners, Paul Biya (1986: 43-47), also envisaged a one party system within a strong state as the most effective strategy at realising the same goal. The New Deal political philosopher believed that democratising a state did not entail weakening it lest it become incapable of averting danger when the integrity of the state is threatened. Nevertheless, Paul Biya's new deal strategy did not envisaged a strategy that protects Cameroonians from foreign interference, meddling, and domination. According to the New Deal political philosophy, the one party option was the only possible instrument of achieving national unity and of rallying efforts and consciousness under the direct control of the state for the realisation of the New Deal programme for nation-building. Nation building is geared essentially towards producing a global citizenship or an interdependent humanity, in response to the wishes of his metropolitan patrons who are the designers and backers of his policies, in exactly the same way as it was the case with his predecessor, Ahmadou Ahidjo.

The major shortfall of Communal Liberalism, first, is its lack of profundity, considering the superficiality in the analytic approach adopted by the author. Secondly, as an African development philosophy, as it claims to be, it is not rooted in an African interpretive framework, which extols the virtues of how knowledge was produced, used and controlled for the attainment of specific end states in any specific African society or in any anthropological reality. It is a political philosophy that is discursive in approach with no attention paid to its practicability as a strategy of engaging the whole population in the struggle against foreign invasion and nation-building. It rather confirms the author's philosophical disposition in which the state is perceived as a partnership between local and foreign governments and international financial institutions, and therefore, not revolutionary against the white man's invasion of Cameroon. Its expressed intentionality to put the economy entirely at the service of the citizens turned out, in practice, to achieve the exact opposite by crippling the economy and dispossessing the citizens under foreign dictatorship. Communal Liberalism, on which the New Deal Programme was based, was a response to an external stimulus and thus had nothing to do with transforming the nation into a self-governing and self-transformational totality.

Considering that the post-colonial political ideas and strategies of realising them have always been determined from outside, the April 6, 1984 failed coup d'état could easily have been masterminded by France to use as a pretext to fortify Paul Biya's presidency and to increase his powers since the foreign designers of the liberalisation programme could predict that its devastations would lead to popular protests. The discontents that did come as a result of the implementation of SAP in the 1990s were managed through the Social Democratic Front (SDF), which itself benefited from the post-cold war politics in the North that included the sponsorship of political movements. Sponsorship of political movements in the late 1980s, towards the end of the Cold War, just before the fall of communism constituted part of the doctrine of liberalisation and democratisation. In Cameroon, following the doctrine of liberalisation and democratisation blowing in from the east following the collapse of communism, the presidency paradoxically emasculated the rest of the political institutions in Cameroon, including the National Assembly, thereby restricting the political sphere, standing out as the strongest political institution in the country. In the final analysis, President Paul Biya's New Deal political philosophy established a free-for-all territory with anarchy as the basis of government, with no clear cut rules. A system which was socially and economically strangulating ordinary citizens. A collaborating stratum received compensation for participation and loyalty to a racket of domination. This came very much close to his political idea of communal liberalism which dovetailed well with the doctrine of liberalisation and democratisation imposed by the IMF/World Bank to achieve a free-for-all economic terrain with foreigners as major actors.

The bottom line is that unlike President Ahmadou Ahidjo who resorted to deploying a strategy that consisted of achieving unity by the whip for subordinating Cameroonians under the European mission to subordinate, exploit and dehumanise, Paul Biya had to bow to the overwhelming pressure from the foreign but powerful partners of the business state. Thus he abandoned his idea of a strong state as the most effective strategy to realize this goal of developing a novel New Deal strategy to democratize and liberalize communal ties. This novel New Deal strategy would have enabled the New deal political philosopher to achieve the same results of subordinating Cameroonians under the new system of things on the international scene in which the European mission to subordinate, exploit and dehumanise had crystallised into a global imperial order following the Washington consensus. Paul Biya had to succumb to pressure from international financial agencies to adopt a strategy that was in line with the language of the day. The language in vogue at the time was the language of democratisation which held was gusting from the east. Cameroonians hailed Paul Biya not only for being smart enough to embrace this fashionable language but for astutely introducing it to Cameroon.

Table 2: Effects of SAP on Cameroon's "Economy"

No	States Corporations Closed	Banks Closed	State Corporations Privatised
1	National Produce Marketing Board	Cameroon Bank	SONEL
2	SODECAO	Crédit Agricole	CDC- Tea Estates
3	Benoue Development Authority	BIAO-Meridien	CDC-Banana Estates
4	FONADER	-	REGIFERCAM
5	ZAPI-EST	-	BICIC
6	National Research Projects	-	HEVECAM
7	CELLUCAM	-	SOCAPALM
8	SODERIM	-	CAMTEL
9	WADA	-	SOCAR
10	AMACAM	-	SNEC
11	CNR	-	CAMSUCO
12	SOTUC	-	CamPost
13	MIDEVIV	-	SCB
14	WESTCORN	-	-
15	SODEBLE	-	-
16	MISSAMBE	-	-
17	CAMAIR	-	-

The table shows the economic consequences that came along with implementation of the New Deal political philosophy the champion of which succumbed to pressure from international financial agencies to adopt a strategy in line with the language of the day in order subordinate Cameroonians to impulses of the global imperial order during a time when strong states were no longer required in Africa. Major trends inherent in the principal political philosophies were complicit with foreign backers of the post-colonial state. These were provoked into being by the persuasive discourse of post-colonialism, wrapped in the post-war discourse of development. That compelled each to adopt a strategy corresponding to Western interest eventually adopting foreign economic structures euphemistically referred to as Cameroon's economy. When these were deliberately destroyed during the 'democratisation' process of the 1990s, which was essentially that of liberalisation, that paved the way for the country to revert to the direct control of foreign backers. Adopting strategies that corresponded to Western interest eventually and adopting foreign economic structures Cameroonians fell into enslavement in service of the survival of the white race. Thus this idea, as an outside initiative backed by force and psychological manoeuvrings, with no counterbalancing force within, has enslaved people, making the situation in Cameroon worse off today than before 1884 when indigenous peoples were free to recreate themselves and their societies in their own image, using their own built-in capacitors in relation to other social systems around them.

Privatisation in Cameroon under the liberalisation agendas of the 1990s, spelled disaster. It achieved the exact opposite of what Cameroonians had expected. A few examples will illustrate this point. Privatisation of the National Railway Corporation (RNCF) cut off the Nkongsamba link. Private owners of the corporation preferred to use old, dilapidated trains and colonial infrastructure for the transportation of goods rather than people since that was more profitable. When the tea sector of the Cameroon Development Corporation (CDC) privatised in 2002, over 1000 workers were immediately retrenched, and those retained had fringe benefits withdrawn with no improvement in living conditions in the camps[5]. Strikes and protests frequently took place in that sector of the CDC immediately after privatisation.

Liberalisation and privatisation brought about conditions similar to those of the colonial era when Europeans invaded Cameroon with a destructive and dehumanising mission. Following both circumstances, ethnic groups seemed the only sure place with communal support for those unlucky enough to avoid being co-opted as middle class collaborators of foreign dehumanising missions. These dehumanising missions tended to strengthen ethno-regional ties, which, in turn, tended to overshadow national solidarity, thereby fragmenting the political sphere Fogui (1990). Furthermore, the imposition of the HIPC initiative in 2000, which successfully killed the Jubilee 2000 campaign for debt cancellation, only postponed Cameroon's heavy indebtedness and its burden of loan repayments. In spite of the rigorous pursuit of strategies of attaining the HIPC completion point and the implementation of poverty reduction programmes, human suffering in Cameroon was further exacerbated.

Thus, any assessment of the achievements or failures of Paul Biya's vision could be misleading since, like his predecessor, he was just a representative of foreign governments and international financial agencies there to exploit the human and natural resources of society regardless of the human and environmental impact. Obviously Paul Biya's policy of liberalisation was intended to attract foreign donors as the authors of *Le Renouveau Cameroun* (1983) put it. His duty was to obey the instructions of his metropolitan patrons, who are the foreign yet extremely powerful partners in nation-building. This is clearly stated in *Communal Liberalism*. Besides that, the transmigration of capital is for financial profit and thus has no social agenda. With no social agenda, the transmigration of

---

[5] For a fuller account of the deplorable living conditions in the plantation camps, see Ardener 1960 and Rudin 1938.

capital has nothing to do with issues of collective interests and can only create economic imbalances. Talk of economic growth only mystifies the processes of production, distribution, and consumption. In this case, invisible hands guide mysteriously beyond the knowledge and control of the majority of Cameroonians who have tended to survive only on hopes since 1957.

Chapter Five

The lethargy of a Post-colonial Political Experiment

Sound knowledge in social manufacturing teaches us that the success or failure of a political experiment depends entirely on the foundation philosophy on which it was laid. This means that the foundation philosophy on which a political experiment is rooted matters a great deal. The previous chapters nave established that Cameroon as a political experiment was not laid on any home-grown foundation philosophy. Not laid on any home-grown foundation philosophy, the power structure in Cameroon has been lethargic hurling Cameroonians from side to side like a wrecked ship on the high seas. The proceeding paragraphs will either falsify or establish the veracity of this hypothesis. Before we move on an evaluation of what the principal political actors in Cameroon had in mind to set up will illuminate the discussion.

Evaluating the Political Philosophies of the Three Principal Political Actors

This evaluation is based on the premise that the effectiveness of a political philosophy depends on whether it is a home-grown political philosophy developed with the intention plough back into its social milieu by putting in place a power structure that nourishes as it self generates. We begin by examining the origins of the very concept of a nation-state out of which the idea of nation-building arose and caught the attention of the principal political philosophers. We begin by asking: what were these political philosophers targeting as an object they intended to realise? The nation-state out of which the notion of nation-building was derived originated in Europe with the French Revolution. The French Revolution of 1778–1779, was a product of the Enlightenment sweeping across Europe in the course of the 18th century. The enlightenment wrested Europe from political anarchy that had become an integral part of Europe's political identity since the fall of the Roman Empire in the 5th century. This legacy took a toll on Africa in the last quarter of the 19th century extending into the 20th century. The French Revolution initiated the idea of a nation-state in Europe. The idea of a nation-state in eighteenth century Europe served as a systematising concept for political power, through which conquest and domination could be attained. For its part, the concept of political power was demonstrated by the Napoleonic wars which seem to have confirmed the power of the nation-state. The Napoleonic wars confirmed the power of the nation-state, which emerged from Westphalia in 1684 and ended the eighty years war between Spain and the Dutch Republic. These wars went further to animate political life in eighteenth century Europe. The nation-state was found to be a useful political instrument of power and control for the subjugation of colonised subjects in Africa as well as in the rest of the colonised societies in the world. This brings home the point that the political philosophers in Cameroon were thinking of realising a project that was implemented in Europe in the 18th century for a purpose quite opposite to what they were eager to achieve. This explains why the nation-building project Cameroon negates the foundation for the nation laid by the social actors themselves. When the social actors themselves decide to lay a foundation for their own nation, they first of all recognise their own very existence as a collection of one people with one vision.

When social actors recognise their own existence as a collection of one people with one vision as Um Nyobe had tried to do just shortly before the idea of immediate independence caught up with the UPC, that justifies and legitimates social and historical action as the social actors undertakes to birth a nation and to set up a realm of political power within it in charge of policy conception and implementation. This did not happen in Cameroon upon the inception of the nation-building project for the realisation of a nation-state. Secondly, and subsequent to the idea just mentioned, the nation-building project did not set out to put in place culture as a system of classification and therefore a knowledge system. Culture as a system of classification and therefore a knowledge system sets the standards for the relationships between the various categories within the structural whole in which the individual, who should be the main social actor and primary beneficiary of his/her actions, is at the originating process of social and historical action as they collectively struggle to keep the nation at equilibrium. This, too, did not happen in Cameroon as well and could explain why tribalism characterised social life in Cameroon during the immediate post-independence period. The temptation of all three main political philosophers was to remove the individual from the originating process of action by treating culture from a superficial angle, limiting their thinking only to the manifest or the observable aspects of it, thereby not treating it as a system that embodies even its socio- structural aspects that emanate from the actions of the individual who create the cultural institutions within which his/her actions are based as he/she seeks to transform his/her world .

The picture they had in mind of a nation-state was a destructive one instead. It was a destructive one in the sense that they sought to destroy the pre-existing knowledge systems and culture to build instead something not rooted on home-grown foundation philosophy. They intended to cultivate this foreign philosophy in order to grow a new nation legitimised by a social contract that should equally constitute the foundation of its structural form, becoming an integral part of its cultural system that determines the social practices within the polity. When it comes to national liberation, however, Um Nyobe stands out matchlessly tall as the symbol of that liberation struggle. When it comes to configuring a transient social space into a nation, he was almost misled, like the other two, by the post-colonial discourses that were narrated in Africa by the ideology of hegemonic dominance, fashionably called modernity. This post-Westphalia type of nation-state was transported into Africa by Europeans. To situate post-colonial studies it is important to understand the birth place of colonisation through which the concept of a nation-state was introduced in Cameroon in particular and among the colonised subjects of the world in general. The birth place of colonisation can be traced back to Westphalia. Westphalia influenced the awkward notion of the nation-state found in Africa today. This awkward notion works against the people in favour of a sovereign ruler who is the *persona civitatis*. The end of the thirty years war fought from 1618 to 1648 in the former lands of the Roman Empire, and the eighty years war from 1568 to 1648, necessitated the peace of Westphalia. This Westphalia peace initiated a new system of sovereignty throughout Europe. This new system of sovereignty based on the adoration of the supremacy of a sovereign ruler over domestic affairs within a bounded territoriality actually constituted the origin of the nation-state. Europeans eventually obligatorily transported this notion to Africa and the rest of the formerly colonised world. This new form of political organisation failed to restore peace in a Europe torn apart by War. Spain and France remained at war for over a decade thereafter. Nevertheless this new form of political organization successfully balanced power by rectifying the imperial power gabs, equalising Protestantism with Catholicism under the law. Religious determinism set afoot by the peace of Augsburg in 1555 solidified. The balance of power throughout the continent of Europe went further than just underpinning religious determinism to actually recognise the right of each nation-state to rule over its own lands and its citizens. Both historical events provoke imperial aspiration into existence. Warring parties took advantage of the new political arrangement to turn their aggressive attitudes outwards into expansive efforts mainly for the purpose of resource exploitation among people. Hugo Grotius (1583-1645) in Law of War and Peace (1625) and

Samuel Pufendorf (1632-1694) in Law of Nature and Nations (1672) gave an intellectual blast to this outward expansive efforts by Europeans. These nations carried out this expansion under the ruse of civilising missions targeting Africa, Asia and the Middle East. Universalism gave birth to the idea of international law or "law of nations". This "law" provided Europeans justification to subordinate those societies that fell under the aggression of European outwards expansive efforts or colonisation. This aggression embodied the evils of European global dominant secular agendas. Over time the coloniser and the colonised became layered in relationships of domination and exploitation. Regrettably, the inception of the post-Westphalia type of nation-state in Africa gave the impression that the nation-building project was in point of fact a project to set up a business enterprise. The understanding of a nation-state as a business enterprise comes through very clearly in the political philosophies of Ahmadou Ahidjo and Paul Biya. What this denotes is that the conception of a nation-state as a business enterprise as it emerged from Westphalia had instead mixed-up Ahmadou Ahidjo and Paul Biya and had in fact unfocused them from that original African leadership task of configuring a transient social space into a nation. In pre-modern African civilization the nation and the form of state structure emerges from social contracts, pacts, or agreements that constitute the foundation of the nation as groups of people seek to reshuffle themselves into larger groups in search of social capital with which to empower themselves to meet their biological and physiological needs in their interactions with the physical world. Nobody is seen as poor *ab initio*. In pre-modern African civilization Africans had conceived of a nation as an entity that emerges from the collective will of all the social actors. These Out of the thoughts and actions of these major actors structures emerge which in turn channel thoughts and actions into productive ends, vital for the survival of the people, becoming the strength of the nation.

Fascinated by the post-colonial discourses that were narrated in Africa by the ideology of hegemonic dominance, stylishly called modernity, motored by the post-Westphalia type of nation-state, Ahmadou Ahidjo and Paul Biya forgot their context of political action. They sought to establish a nation based on a foundation philosophy derived from a foreign land with a foreign agenda. In this way they created a structure that was linked to an external source. This dynamic contravened the universality of the laws that regulate the creation of structures as Claude Levi-Strauss maintains. Claude Levi-Strauss has maintained that for a structure to qualify as one that structure must be a self-regulatory and a self-transformational whole. Based on the universality of laws that regulate the creation of structures it would be inadmissible that the thinking of the nation should negate the procedure by which the foundation for the nation is laid by the social actors themselves. Um Nyobe succeeded very immensely in stating the problem that whites had invaded and were destroying the material resources of Cameroon and enslaving the people in the process. Nevertheless, he almost fell into this trap when he talked of broadening the economic base to engage the poorer masses of the population and weaving the various cultural matrices to produce a national culture. The Cameroonian people ought to have been given the freedom to socially order or reorder themselves into a political structure with its unique cultural system emanating from a well-grounded knowledge base that nourishes a home-grown foundation philosophy. The Cameroonian people should have thus created a political form in its wholeness that derived from and meets their needs and aspirations, depending on the terms of the social engagements undertaken.

Ahmadou Ahidjo and Paul Biya, whose political thoughts have been experimented in Cameroon, denied the Cameroonian people the fundamental freedom of creating a political structure grown from their own actions. Instead they almost single-handedly created a political structure that excluded a large majority of the population who became marginal people living at the periphery of political action, thereby becoming poor and "ignorant" on that basis since they lost control over their own lives and over their physical world. Their world reverted to the "state" and its foreign partners under ambiguous conditions. For that very reason, the people of Cameroon also lost control over the factors of production following the putting in place of a superordinate state structure that depended on an external source for some of its elements in this case financing, defying the whole idea of Cameroon emerging as a structural whole.

This large majority did not and still do not understand what is going on; they lost touch with the "grammar" of politics. They just saw and still see things happening above their heads; they became passive spectators to a few individuals who incarnated the state, seemingly representing foreign interests as their actions tend to reveal, in whose hands the fate of the entire population depends. With the "coming" of the nation-state all the people of Cameroon knew was that the concept of work had changed within the "nation-state". Like a business enterprise, the state set out to mobilise and recruit young people to "work" for the "enterprise of the state" within institutions created not by the people themselves. In the minds of the people, the building of a nation entails citizens *working* for the state and depending entirely on the money derived from their *working* life within a state that was not a self-transformational structural whole but a continuum of foreign organisations with supervening powers over it. This was something new in Africa where almost everybody in the pre-colonial nations, including state functionaries, were never disengaged from the production process[14.] t Tragically orientation to this practice became a condition sine qua non for the abandonment of old identities awkwardly styled national unity and later on as national integration.

However, a closer examination of the political thoughts of the three main actors quickly reveal some common themes running through them such as that of unity and the centrality of a strong state structure in national political life. One hypothesis to explain this phenomenon is that Um Nyobe, in his struggle against the European invaders, had outlined and laid the essential framework for national liberation, independence and nation-building in Cameroon. As such, it is possible that the pro-Europeans in collaboration with the European armed robbers themselves, (they both had and used armies equipped with high fire power), who destroyed the national liberation movement and eliminated its leaders, adopted much of it. It is possible they adopted much of it only to gain a veneer of nationalism they badly needed to legitimise their actions. Secondly, they must have adopted it as a strategy to douse the seething flames of nationalism or simply to use it as an instrument to entice the masses for subjugation. This was possible at a time when the Public Service had cropped up and was promising employment and money for all. Unfortunately, they did so with no intention to implement it or at least not to implement it with the same target as originally designed by the genuine national liberation movement. By so doing they indeed captured the country for the European global invaders under a strong state. Under a strong state, they imposed an obnoxious notion of unity on the people of Cameroon whom they suppressed with the use of the army and marginalised them by the use of the law.

This may explain the reasons for the similarity in some key elements in the various political philosophies but it does not readily explain why their application by subsequent "nation-builders" achieved the opposite effect, nor does it say if Um Nyobe would have achieved the same result had he succeeded. To draw a sweeping conclusion that the implementation of the political ideas, successively by the last two "nation-builders", has been unsuccessful because they were characteristically inadequate, and inadequate because they were poorly conceived, could be misleading. The historical processes and social context in which a political philosophy is implemented is also important in determining its success or failure. In this case, a political philosophy would be said to have succeeded when it has confirmed the social milieu and would have failed when it is at variance with the social milieu in which it is being experimented, especially when it does not derive from the social milieu itself. In Cameroon political thinking has never been rooted on the Cameroonian social milieu with the intention of creating a home-grown world view. This world view should become the foundation philosophy for the thoughts and actions of the people who must not look elsewhere for their *social becoming* but should depend on their own ingenuity for everything. There was no intention to build a whole self-transformational social structure but rather to create an open society that exposes its elements to foreign influences some of which are disastrous. What is it that the post-World War II concept of *development* sought to achieve that Cameroonian people cannot achieve by themselves? If people need a road they will construct it and if they see a need to ply the seas they will invent a way of doing so. Why must people be made to see development only as coming from somewhere else and not being the result of their own actions if this does not serve someone's interest somewhere?

Cameroon puts on lipstick like a woman only to persuade "foreign partners" with whom state officials collude to enslave Cameroonians. This makes the structure shaky and leaky. The current pattern of *development* follows what the state and its foreign partners consider as priority areas with local people participating in the process only to thank "almighty government" for giving them development. Most often too this is attributed to the lack of means. But where do means come from? The problem with Cameroon is not that of the lack of means but that of Cameroon being a transition zone for foreign capital, which comes in only to enslave Cameroonians and fly back to European countries. The brewery companies (about 99 percent foreign owned), for example, brew an average of about five million barrels or hectolitres of beer annually for the intoxication of Cameroonians who spend their time and money drinking rather than thinking and strategizing. This yields an annual beer consumption rate per person of about 3.125 litres.

In financial terms, this annual consumption amounts to FCFA 2.187.500 per person expenditure on European bottled beer. This constitutes a major source of currency repatriation to European countries since those brewery companies are affiliates of multi-nationals. Beer consumption actually constitutes not only an economic risk for Cameroonians but a health hazard as well. Alcohol consumption in recent decades is a major contributing factor in the skyrocketing rates of non-communicable diseases (NCDs). In Cameroon NCDs accounted for 43% of total deaths in 2002. If those brewing companies along with other major industries in Cameroon, were indigenous businesses these huge amounts of money could tar all the roads in Cameroon and do much more and would empower Cameroonians to do away with NCDs. Imagine a situation where such colossal sums of money were invested in Cameroon in productive ends. Cameroonians would be able to tar their roads and stay healthy at the same time while eliminating a major public health problem – NCDs. Yet Cameroonians prefer to participate in the enterprise of currency repatriation to the white man countries only to complain of poverty.

In the petroleum sector, about ten European companies jointly exploit the petroleum sector, shielded by SONARA (the National Oil Refinery Corporation). NONARA produces heavy crude while Cameroonians buy light crude from their fuel stations very expensively with money that trickles upwards to Europe, leaving Cameroon as a petroleum producing country. Paradoxically Cameroon remains a poor country according to criteria adopted by the World Bank. This is just what a leaky social structure that lacks its own self-transformational laws does to its people simply because the people were denied the freedom of creating their own self-governing institutions within which to act by themselves to transform their world[15].

---

[15] All human beings have a mobilisational capacity. Unfortunately the power structure in Cameroon was created to restrict Cameroonians from

A significant omission in all the three political philosophies is the failure to give consideration to the pre-existing institutions and the ideals they produce and propagate. These institutions served as the nexus of society for the production and maintenance of bonds of solidarity. They also served as tools of social and political organisation and cultural reproduction and regeneration for the pre-existing ethno-polities. They based political philosophies on floating concepts and false assumptions – assumptions not grounded on the reality of their social milieu. This results in attempts to talk down to people with no consideration for their pre-existing situation as if people were non-beings who did not know how to put meaning to their lives. The three political philosophers treated culture from an unrealistic perspective, focusing attention only on the manifest aspects of culture, namely; music, drama, drawing, art and craft, neglecting the fact that culture includes the non-material, which is the process of integrating both the spiritual and the physical elements into one anthropo-social whole for the binding, regulating and determining of social behaviour, and not something that can be displayed for assessment or for entertainment. As Foucault (1970) puts it, those manifest forms are only an expression, that is to say; a symbolic disclosure of the inner laws that govern the order of being including its language and its social structure. Consequently, they gave no room for Cameroonians from below to build their own nation

---

mobilizing themselves and realizing projects that are vital for the transformation of their world. As a matter of fact, the mobilisational capacity of Cameroonians is being directed towards wasteful ends. With the mobilisational capacity of Cameroonians directed towards wasteful ends Cameroonian tend to realize projects which are not politically and economically strategic. It should be recalled that by way of electricity cables the economy of Cameroon is subordinated to that of the USA. This is supported by the government through its policy of privatisation which ties with the government's concept of development. Privatisation, for example that favours foreign companies discourages all initiatives that may lead to a change in the status quo in favour of Cameroonians gaining economic independence.

from the roots, in their own image, seeing culture only from the perspective of Western education. Nevertheless, culture goes further than that. Plagiarised versions of the national liberation political philosophies of Ahmadou Ahidjo and Paul Biya reveal that they did not derive from their social milieu. While the original basic outlines by Um Nyobe remained the same, the structural significant differences lie in their emphasis on employing a foreign element. This also includes the emphasis on financing which is the carrier of all ills that emanate from the Western industrial societies including social and environmental ills. This points to a possibility of achieving results that are external to the very structure they were struggling to set up. Another hypothesis that readily explains the lacklustre presentation of the last two political philosophies is that, unlike that of Um Nyobe, which was found to be rooted on an anti–invasion thought, the other two were based on the intentions to collaborate with the imperialists oppressors rather than on the will to oppose them. When the enemy controls the processes of adaptation opposing them while adopting their systems and ideologies is a political impossibility.

This is very visible in the political agenda of these new bureaucratic aristocrats, who target means of consumption and pleasure seeking which is dominated by the politics of money which they euphemistically call democracy. In the school of thought of those who sought to collaborate with the oppressors, democracy is just a means to mislead the population to believe that the longing for foreign capital though important and the spread of Western systems is what national liberation and nation-building is all about. Hence, they failed to target means of production and to encourage massive indigenous capital accumulation and investment and the emergence of a broad-based ideological and structural framework for political development. They have demonstrated a lack of a genuine intention to put in place a mechanism that can enable Cameroonians to interact among themselves for the emergence of a national language and a national culture as they relate with the physical world. Both Ahmadou Ahidjo and Paul Biya in their quest for foreign partners forgot that a nation is built by the individuals themselves acting in concert through social engagements to define the lives of each of their individual members within processes of institutional formation and adaptation define by the individuals themselves. They also forgot that a nation is built by setting in motion processes that ensure the embedding of social aggregates as new social formations keep emerging within territorial units of their own and not through decrees emanating from an executive desk. Ethnic particularisms have remained a recurring feature in Cameroon. Cultural and development associations sprouted and flourished under the regimes of both Ahmadou Ahidjo and Paul Biya since they both successively preferred to use superficial approaches in imposing parallel structures on the pre-existing ethno-polities out of which Cameroon was supposed to have emerged as the product of a social contract with its unique cultural identity.

Instead of Cameroon emerging as a product of a social contract with its unique cultural identity, Ahmadou Ahidjo enacted a state of emergency law in 1960 under which he was able to beat up Cameroonians, killing and imprisoning many thousands, forcing them to accept an illegality imposed by France and submit themselves to slavery without question. That was how Cameroon emerged as a post-colonial state. Following the emergence of Cameroon as a post-colonial state, Ahmadou Ahidjo called on Cameroonians to abandon their ethnic identities and adopt only the "Cameroon identity". Unfortunately, what he meant by a "Cameroon identity" was not a result of the systematic composition and re-composition of the pre-existing ones but rather a destruction of them in preference of a vague and formless identity emerging from an arbitrary process. Between 1960 and the early 1980s the pre-existing ethnic groups held themselves together in fear under a reign of terror as Ahmadou Ahidjo single-handedly played his ethnic and regional arithmetic positioning and repositioning ethno-regional groupings the way he liked claiming that what he was doing was regional balancing. Regrettably regional balancing was his idea of redistributing the slave wages among the various groupings. Following the liberalisation laws of the 1990s under Paul Biya ethno-regional groupings abandoned fear and sought to express themselves in public and so could ask for their own share of the "bread of sorrow". This constituted a veritable source of ethnic tensions, clearly portraying Cameroon not as an auto-regulating totality that should be characteristic of a structural whole. Ethnic tensions were an indication that Cameroon was but a mere collection of social aggregates fitted into a geographical space employing external elements then yielding results external to it as well lacking mechanism for self-regulation. Cameroon emerged into existence as a slave camp, from Ahmadou Ahidjo to Paul Biya. The thinking has been to manipulate and juxtapose social aggregates by holding the ethno-regional groupings captive in their positions as immutable and non-interactional units. There has been no intention to give room for populations to reshuffle and to recompose themselves in a process that can lead to a self-regulating structural whole with people themselves as the main actors. Ever since post-colonial Cameroon emerged in history not as a self-regulating structural whole but as a mere collection of social aggregates, the tendency has been for a single individual to claim to lead the whole population. So called leaders overwhelmed the people with the post-colonial discourse of developmentalism part of the lustful drive for modernisation under a highly militarized state that keeps people waiting indefinitely, waiting to become what they will never become.

Those who were estranged and displaced from their ethnic groups, where they had the right to social support and means of production and who had moved out to offer their labour either in the civil service, industries or plantations soon realised that what was called Cameroon was actually a transient entity, deftly dovetailed into the European economic structure, operating as a sub system for the transmission of the European values under European implanted and ill adapted structures, which have been self-style as being those of modernity. Such a European implanted and ill adapted admixture did not show any sign of a genuine intention of a mechanism to define their lives in the same way as did the pre-existing institutions and world views within the ethno-political units. Under the post-colonial arrangement, the ethno-political units still stand today in opposition to Cameroon, which is rather a vague concept that originated from Westphalia in the seventeenth century and found itself in Africa out of a bargain the people of Africa did not make. Within it, the socially atomised estranged and displaced from their ethnic groups, left to look for a means of survival under the new arrangement, resorted to a practice of regrouping themselves in the "diaspora" based on ethnic filiations (cultural and development associations). Cultural and development associations in Cameroon constituted the basis of ethnic particularisms and were reinforced by the ethno-regional approach to politics adopted by the two regimes. In Cameroon even today, appointments to posts of responsibility in government follow this principle. In their mad rush to achieve national unity or national integration, by bringing the ensemble of the people of the territory under servitude for the metropolitan powers, the last two aristocratic bureaucrats treated people as though they were floating social atoms, separated from the physical world. This approach only helped to dispossess and enslave the citizens of this country. They forgot to work out a strategy on how Cameroon, as a country, as a people, not the state, would acquire land, around which the reshuffling of the population would constitute the basis of a gradual process for socio-cultural integration. The state treated the owners of the land as none beings imposing its will on them without their consent, appropriating their land with the use of legislation, carrying on the colonial approach to land acquisition by the state.

According to the minutes of a meeting to settle a land dispute between Bambui and Finge, of January 23, 1960, Premier J.N. Foncha said that "there was no empty space in Cameroon since all land was owned". This implied that the new state, which came into existence not as a result of the owners of the land recomposing themselves into a bigger polity, but through the 'good will gesture' of a European country, sanctioned by a European controlled international organisation. The state was in an ambiguous position to claim rights of ownership over any land. Of course this could be possible only by a land legislation that systematically denies citizens free access to land. Why should Cameroonians buy land, much less pay land taxes, or on rents in what is supposed to be their own country? Cameroonians should be the beneficial owners of the physical world within their national territory, which should constitute the basis for the establishment of social and political institutions necessary for self-preservation and self-replacement which is the basis of life itself. Under no circumstance should the state compete with citizens in land ownership let alone deprive citizens of land use. History should embody the actions of all individuals (every single individual is a historical being) within the state and not only a few who are claiming to be acting on behalf of the people.

Unfortunately, the practice of estrangement that emerged out of the colonial internal labour migration process, which has turned Cameroonians into existentialists, has become a normal trajectory for human evolution. For one thing unity is not achieved from behind an executive desk in a process of arbitrary intermixture of "floating social atoms" through the Public Service nor by the imposition of parallel structures on pre-existing ones backed by a foreign-adopted legislation that curtails people's freedom to reshuffle themselves in relation to their material world. It is achieved by the people themselves uniting around certain key values through which they are able to attain the three goals of life, namely; the primary, secondary, and tertiary goals all by themselves in a dialectical interaction with their physical world as they seek to transform it thus transforming their lives by themselves. In short, attempts to decree a country into existence in Cameroon has proven to be unworkable, lethargic.

In the final analysis we realise that the political philosophy of Paul Biya, like that of Ahmadou Ahidjo before him, was centred on collaboration with European invaders. All they professed was just rigmarole of the plagiarised version of what was outlined by Um Nyobe who intended to unite the country under a strong state as a strategy not aimed at taking away the autonomy of the individual but for the eviction of the European invaders from the country. While Ahmadou Ahidjo adopted a statist strategy, which combined social provisioning, service delivery system, and economic management, all by the state that was repressive in character in which the administrative cadre, in the absence of an established political ideology and indigenous capital, played a pragmatic role under the close supervision of France. Paul Biya, for his part, while adopting the same strategy (Biya 1986: 47, 116) rather disengaged the state from social provisioning, service delivery system, and economic management in which the administration, while still retaining the repressive instruments of the state, which were put in place by the invading Europeans (the military, the gendarmerie, the police, the judiciary, and the penitentiary), played a deregulatory role in a liberalised economy under the close supervision of international financial institutions, recording an economic growth rate of 4 % as opposed to the 7 % of the Ahmadou Ahidjo era.

But this is not to say that Ahmadou Ahidjo succeeded more than Paul Biya, for the economic growth rate was based on floating capital and the assessment itself was done by foreign financial organisations to justify their never-ending interventions in their profit seeking motives. Hence the rigorous pursuit of money from foreign sources by the last two "nation-builders"; by satisfying the demands of foreign governments and foreign institutions did not favour the development of a national culture and a national language emerging with it. In their rigorous pursuit of money from foreign sources for the building of infrastructure, which has been mistaken for the birthing of a nation, "nation builders" forgot the social actors, or at least used them only as a means to an end (slaves). They forgot that the social actors came into the project, though involuntarily, with their own languages. Emmanuel N. Chia asserts that these languages constituted the data for their collective experiences in their various cultural domains, including health, agriculture, communications, technological fields, etc. These should have been maintained for national development and not suppressed in favour of colonial languages (Chia 2006: 117, 126). The "nation builders" also forgot the indigenous people's original conception of human nature and its process of evolution, which was wrapped up in their spiritual life, defined and expressed through their various linguistic inventions, which they tended to suppress in favour of unrealistic colonial forms of expression. In so doing they left out the necessary building material in the nation-building project, rendering their political philosophies grossly inadequate. Consequently, the option for the pursuit of a foreign element in the task of building a structure by this voracious class, which replaced the nationalists, mitigates their intentions and efforts at achieving a structure in its wholeness, together with its transformation laws, and which is capable of auto-regulation and auto-modernisation.

Both Jean Piaget and Claude Levi-Strauss, as well as other structuralists, point out that the wholeness of a structure cannot be achieved by relying or depending on a foreign element in the process of its composition. George Balandier refers to this as an external dynamic, which can turn be disruptive to the very system it purports to create. Allain Touraine in his concept of historicity maintains that a higher or superior society assisting a lower or inferior one in the processes of its evolution is a mystification of the fact about structuration. According to Allain Touraine's concept of historicity, every society has the capacity to give itself an orientation and to act on that orientation to transform itself, a thing the last two fake and mentally corrupt "nation-builders" failed to consider in their nation-building political philosophies. Although arguing within the context of civil society or neo-institutional groups McDonald and Warburton (2003: 383) advances a theoretical corpus that is supportive of Alain Touraine's theory. They contend that when people create structures themselves with no extraneous influences; (1) the modes of operation within the institutions that ensure the maintenance and persistence of the social structure takes a taken-for-granted quality; (2) participants develop a language, it's the long usage of which develops their interpretative framework and establishes a legitimate basis for their thoughts and actions, shaping their behaviour pattern accordingly; (3) the long active involvement of the participants in the process of organisational socialisation, considering their similarity of backgrounds, creates and sustains a high degree of normative and ideological consensus fundamental for the institutionalisation of the social structure. Of course, the process for the composition or formation of a superstructure in the name of Cameroon was initiated by the interventions of foreign illegal European invaders and their agencies, which, since then, have never stopped their interventions on the structure they imposed on the people.

This has made it impossible for the creation of a normative and an ideological consensus fundamental for the smooth composition of the structural framework where modes of operation take on a taken-for-granted quality with social actors developing for themselves a language. This consensus should become the legitimate basis of their thoughts and actions, being the store of their collective social memory, acquired through the processes of their interactional engagements among themselves and with their physical world as they struggle to develop a national cultural identity. Dependence on a foreign element as Balandier puts it, has been disruptive to all attempts at creating a social structure in Cameroon. We now turn to understanding the background to the phenomenon that has subjected Cameroon to a situation of dependence.

Background to Imposed Dependence

The invasion and exploitation of Africa in the 19th century by the Europeans was a direct outcome of the European Enlightenment thought of the 17th century. From an uninformed premise, the Enlightenment thought that was sweeping across seventeenth century Europe in fact ignorantly divided the world into two antagonistic categories of people, the world's "civilised" people and the world's "savage" peoples. This uninformed difference was systematised both ideologically and structurally with a policy orientation intended to keep the "savage" Africans permanently under the burden of domination and enslavement by the self-styled "civilised" Europeans. Ideologically, it followed many decades of conceptualisation and publicising. This eventually crystallised into political tools for imperialism during the European quest for political economic, cultural, social, and ecological expansion in the post-radical invention periods of the seventeenth to the nineteenth centuries.

The turbulent nature of Europe was characterised by social ills and wars and a rapid economic and technological development in the 19th century. This favoured economic, political, military, and linguistic expansion, with European countries competing to outsmart each other in the scramble among themselves and subsequently for colonies among the "savage" people with basically economic intentions (Tanjutek 1998: 40-57). A dichotomous global economic order established exploitative relations of production as Claude (Ake 1978) demonstrates. According to the logic of this dichotomous global economic order with exploitative relations of production, the colonised societies of the "savages" served as peripheral outpost feeders to the metropolitan economic empires. These constituted the basis of a social thought crystallised around the "civilisation" theory and animated the historical and political actions of Europeans towards the other races of the world, especially Africans whom they described as "primitive" people who occupied lower rungs of civilisation.

The civilisation theory was given a push by the social evolutionist theories of the older generation of European intellectuals such as Hubert Spencer and Auguste Comte who proposed linear three stage linear theory of evolution that purports that progress was from the inferior to the superior stage. This view of human progress received further intellectual support from the distinctions made to social categories by Emile Durkheim (organic and mechanical solidarity), Ferdinand Tönnies' *Geselschaft* and *Gemeinschaft*. These all nourished the basis of a prejudicial view of Africans by Europeans and conventionalised a dichotomous or bipolar world order of superior whites versus the inferior blacks. Worst still, Talcott Parson's introduction of a world system approach to the study of society, as evolving from simple to complex or evolving from a primitive state and gradually getting civilized over time, finally divided the world's people into the inferior natives and the superior Europeans. Equating the culture and technology of Western civilization with progress the pompous division of the world into that of the inferior natives and the superior Europeans,Talcott Parson presupposed that the 'old' African world must be condemned and destroyed. Talcott Parson's introduction of a world system approach to the study of society unfortunately served as the last nail on the coffin as it laid the foundation for the formulation of modernization as a development theory. Modernization as a development theory regrettably evolved into an ideology of hegemonic dominance with the struggle for existence as its implicit key component.

With the struggle for existence having become an implicit key component of the ideology of hegemonic dominance, imperialism had to produce objectives and physical results to be meaningful within its context. Accordingly, international institutions such as the United Nations, especially after the post-World War II period, played a decisive role by subjecting African societies under European states through the famous chapter 76 of the UN Charter. Zang-Atangana describes this as indirect manipulation. While those international institutions such as the

United Nations played an indirect role in the process of European global invasion, the European states themselves did the direct invasion and destruction (Zang-Atangana (1989: 92), backed by the UN Charter. Having reinforced this objectified world view about the other, the colonial administrators and soldiers then targeted the uncivilised people of the world for manipulation, exploitation and destruction. It was in this context that missionaries too had situated their activities. Acting as part of the civilising mission, the early European missionaries targeted the cultural and ecological spheres for destruction (ibid: 90). A complex combination of both factors ensured the success of the white man's mission to Africa, which was to steal, kill and to destroy.

Its economic motivation was captured in the declaration by French Prime Minister Jules Ferry (1832-1892). As Europe was poised for global invasion, Jules Ferry, in his capacity as French Prime Minister, declared that "colonial policy was the daughter of industrial policy". This declaration eventually became the foundation of French policy of invading and plundering non-European societies for French economic expansion. With an uniformed division of the world into two antagonistic categories off inferior natives on the one hand and superior Europeans on the other, having become a way of understanding the world in Europe, its social underpinnings were echoed in the declaration by the British Prime Minister Lord Salisbury (1830-1930). Qualifying the other races of the world as "dying races," British Prime Minister Lord Salisbury, said that "the white race was to replace the other races of the world" (Noble et al 1994: 964). Rudyard Kipling (1865-1936) in a celebrated poem in favour of imperialism, "White Man's Burden" (1899), captured the essence of European motives for colonialism, which gained inspiration from social Darwinism. Rudyard Kipling's celebrated poem, "white man's burden," enhanced the drive for imperialism (Noble ibid: 966), and constituted the basis of its ideological and structural instruments, political domination and oppression and practically ripped the world apart into categories of exploiters and the exploited. In the particular case of France, Cameroon fell into the category of *"colonies des plantations ou d'exploitations"*, which Roberts (1963: 34) says was the crux of the French colonial policy. Cameroon being the crux of the French colonial policy became the hub of French activities in that region of Africa that became known as the Equatorial Africa. This required a system of imposed dependence wherein

> "not only were the colonies made to pay the total cost of colonial administration but the general aim of French [colonial] rule was to be as "economical" as possible which meant building up reserve funds from the colonies to be used and invested within the metropole …As for Gaullism, it was particularly in the lookout for vassals on which it could perch to enhance its international status (Mongo Beti 1978: 94).

Nation-building as a logical sequence to follow the regaining what Cameroonians had lost, was expected to have been firmly anchored on visions with programmes and strategies that revolutionarily countered this European destructive mode of thinking and acting as a prerequisite to socially reversing it and building a totally new society from the ashes of its practices. Unfortunately, this was not to be the case as neo-colonial agents were to surface on the scene. France especially played a determining role in the decolonisation process (Chaffard 1967) by creating and sustaining a class of a local collaborative stratum of nationalist whom they imposed on Cameroonians to extend French sovereignty on Cameroon. This trend gave rise to what classical economists may describe as the infrastructural base of Cameroon's economy.

Table 3: Trends in the foreign Origins of the infrastructural base of Cameroon's Economy Base

No	Corporation	Year of creation	By	Country of origin
1	German Estate (became CDC in 1947)	1885	Woerman & Jantzen und Thormalen	Germany
2	ALUCAM	1958	Péchiney Ugine	France
3	Douala International Airport	1935	-	France
4	CFDT (became SODECOTON in 1974)	1951	-	France
5	GICAM	1957	-	France
6	CEMENCAM	-	-	France
7	SEREPCA	1952		France

Table shows the colonial origins of the infrastructural base of Cameroon's economy.

The difference between the local collaborate stratum of nationalist and the genuine nationalist who initiated the project for decolonisation is that while the later were assassinated by the French in the *Maquis* (resistance movement against colonial rule), the former were propped up by France. Consequently, President Ahmadou Ahidjo, like his successor President Paul Biya, stayed alive to implement policy prescriptions designed in the metropolis. To be fair they were selected based on a willingness following Cameroon's independence negotiated on private terms between General Charles de Gaulle and Ahmadou Ahidjo. Consequently:

> "The government of Ahmadou Ahidjo did not have to "find its way" in economic matters; the path it has to follow had been carefully planned and laid out since 1946. Moreover, for several years after independence, French experts not only draw up the "development plans", but were able to ensure that the country continues in the "right direction" by their predominance as "advisers" in all the government's economic ministries as well as within Ahidjo's

ruling circle. Under the aegis of FIDES, and FAC tens of billions of Franc CFA were invested by France in Cameroon between 1947 and 1966" (Joseph ibid: 32, 33).

That laid the groundwork for foreign direct investment in Cameroon. Foreign direct investment brought about a strong presence of multinationals in Cameroon's economy. In that extraverted economic arrangement, France alone had about 33 enterprises, constituting 52 per cent of enterprises of European origins that were established in Cameroon before 1981 (See Cameroon Tribune N° 8804 of Thursday 08, March 2007). President Ahmadou Ahidjo enthroned in Cameroon by the French had to tailor his political philosophy for nation-building in Cameroon accordingly. To tailor his political philosophy for nation-building in Cameroon in line with the prevailing circumstances, he had to depend on French aid and expertise and military logistics to coerce innocent people into submission. Illustrating with the cases of long independent countries of South America, and those of Ethiopia and Liberia, which have failed to achieve the goal of nation development with the use of foreign capital, Abel Eyinga argues that Cameroon could not have done any better. "Basing the economy of a country as Ahidjo planned to continue doing in 1958 – 1982 on an eager pursuit of foreign capital simply meant condemning the country to permanent underdevelopment" (Eyinga 1978: 131). Abel Eyinga traces the origins of planned Liberalism in Cameroon as derivative of General de Gaulle's doctrine of "participation". This doctrine blended capitalism and socialism, coined for Cameroon and Gabon by French investors and technical advisers. Ahidjo in 1965 adopted this as a strategy for his economic policy, which avers the obsessional pursuit of foreign capital (ibid: 137).

Moreover, "in contrast to the other French African "possessions" Cameroon had the status of a mandate granted by the *société de nations* to France and so was subjected to various external controls. This vulnerability to an international scrutiny had a number of consequences on the functioning of the Cameroonian labour market" (Clignet 1980: 330), over which the political realm played a supervisory role as designed and directed from abroad. The model of planned liberalism applicable in Cameroon and Gabon was also applicable in other French colonial territories of Cote d'Ivoire, Niger, Central African Republic, Senegal, etc. Though under different appellations these models of planned liberalism designed in France intended to link the economy of the periphery to that of the metropolis (Woungly-Massaga 1984: 118). Indeed, "when examined closely the three plans since independence are actually documents intended to attract [foreign] businessmen and inform them of the different domains in which they are able with the government's protection, to realise excellent profits" (Eyinga ibid: 138,139). The top brass of the UPC had described the development plans as a mystification intended to deceive the people of Cameroon with the political structure playing the game of the imperialist (in Zang-Atangana 1989: 120). This concept of development plans falls within the general mainstay of what was referred to as development. Hargreaves (1996: 29) has said the intention was to manage the power of the colonial state over African lives in order to reinvigorate the periphery.

Thus, President Ahmadou Ahidjo, as a neo-colonialist, spent his tenure of office (1958-1982), under international scrutiny implementing French economic plans in Cameroon. French economic plans in Cameroon were designed by French private concerns and experts under the *Fonds d'Investissement pour le Développement Economique* et Social de la France *d'Outre-mer* (FIDES) programme of development in 1964 as a means to integrating the economies of the ensemble of the French union and to link them to that of the metropolis. With France throttling the economy from behind the scene, President Ahmadou Ahidjo had to renege on his concept of African socialism, which he announced before his party's congress in 1962. The sad thing about Cameroon as a post-colonial arrangement is that even when power changed hands in 1982, the structure of international politics had changed and international institutions were playing a different ball game as we now see.

International Institutions as Tools of Exploitation and Domination

The late 1980s in Cameroon under President Paul Biya who had taken over the mantle of command from Ahmadou Ahidjo corresponded to a period in which the cold war was coming to an end. President Paul Biya took over at a time when international institutions determined the realities of power in the world. The period for 'control' in which one European country subjugated one African country was over. Hence colonised societies, particularly those in Africa were liberalised from the "ownership" of one European country and made to adjust to accommodate a horde of actors. Ahmadou Ahidjo had played his role to conquer and control Cameroon for enslavement by France and was no longer needed. Paul Biya was foisted to play a different role in 'adjusting' the structure of Cameroon to accommodate international capital coming through a multitude of sources. It was a period described as expanding democracy, liberal democracy at that, when rich and powerful Western Europe and North America created and used international institutions to co-ordinate policies T *Third world* countries are used as regions of surplus generation for the metropolis as well as pools for experts for the monitoring of regimes that are under obligation to adjust to the conditionalities imposed on them by these rich and powerful Western States (Keohane and Nye 1993: 2). Rich and powerful states of Western Europe and North America created and used international institutions to co-ordinate their policies and also used them as a block buster for their ability to exploit the resources of the *third world* countries. They also used them to determine the institutional terms of benefits.

> "The end of the second [world] war in 1945.... witnessed not only the dominos collapse of the [Western] "empires" and the end of the occupation of the [third] world nations one after another in the last fifty years. It also saw the establishment of a series of international organisations, institutions, agencies, groups, installations and whatever by the [Western World] to replace their loss of physical presence especially in their former occupied lands and in the [third world] in general. The ultimate and ulterior motive behind these [Western World's] set-ups was and is to maintain their firm control on the economic resources of the [third] world nations, which the [Western World] had exploited for the last 500 years. The worst addition to the [Western world's] curse was that they now use these international organisations, like the United Nations, IMF and World Bank, as vehicles or tools for their neo-colonialism, economic exploitation or "white slavery" and international terrorism" (Tanjutek 1998: 359).

This means that, after World War II, "international" institutions have provided the imperial West in their imperial mission with the institutional framework through which to regain an indirect but firm control over the colonised world assisted by a local collaborating stratum.

> "The period after World War II was much richer in international institutions, principally because the United States exercised a consistent and sustained leadership, partly in reaction to the failure of its policy after World War I. American wartime planning emphasised the significance of establishing new organisations for the provision of regulation of international finance, such as the International Monetary Fund (IMF) and the World Bank, the basis of which was negotiated at Bretton Woods in 1944" (Keohane and Nye ibid : 18).

Consequently, "In 1970 there were 7,000 [multi-national corporations], while in 2003 there was an estimated 63,000 parent companies operating with around 69,000 subsidiaries in all sectors, countries and industries in the world"[16]. Yet there exists no legislation to enforce them to be socially and environmentally responsible. Within this institutional framework, the IMF/World Bank played a decisive role in synchronising the industrial economics while opening up the economies of "less developed" countries for destruction by the rich industrial countries (Noble et al. 1994: 1210).

The World Bank in its World Development Report of 1996, entitled *From Plan to Market,* announced an era of salvation that will follow the state's abandonment of planning. This inadvertently led to the total recapture of the economies of non-European societies, especially in Africa, by the market concerns of European countries that had imposed the World Bank's structural adjustment prescriptions on them.

Accordingly, the memorable issue of epic proportions with disastrous consequences that characterised President Paul Biya's tenure of office was the implementation of the Structural Adjustment Plan (SAP) of the late 1980s. Deplorably, this was followed by the implementation of programmes geared towards poverty alleviation. Regrettably for President Paul Biya, he hardly had finished elaborating his New Deal political philosophy, which is also enshrined in *Communal Liberalism,* which proposes a society free from foreign dictatorship, when on July 1, 1987, the World Bank/IMF, all UN specialised agencies, imposed SAP on Cameroon alongside 38 other African countries. This was a conditionality that "States must accept as a condition for not being ostracised from the world economy. SAP was a package which included privatisation and market

---

[16] "Behind the Mask", a contribution by Christian Aid to knowledge on the hidden agenda behind the concept of cooperate Social Responsibility (CSR), which is currently being peddled by Northern governments and business.

liberalisation, aimed at opening up the economies of less developed societies for reinvasion by the powerful nations of the world notably Western industrial economies though China took advantage of this opening to make its strong presence felt on the global scene and in Africa in particular.

This occurred at a period when international capital was globalising within an institutional framework, which assured its effective regulation both in the West and abroad. This found its origins in the fact that, "the United States had... declined in relative strength from the unprecedented pre-eminence it had enjoyed after World War II... In terms of productivity and living standards, the United States was [also] in relative decline" (Noble et al ibid: 1205). Its economy needed revitalising and the USA also needed a consensus within a context where Western Europe was integrating into a united and powerful bloc. What compounded matters at this point was the fact that some countries like Japan and Germany circumscribed during the cold war were trying to reposition themselves to play leading roles in the international arena.

With these fundamental changes in the structure of international politics,"[t]he United States [which] successfully created international institutions to maintain a congenial political-economic order in Europe ... sought to maintain a complex of interests that had formed around institutions that it had itself created "(Keohane et al. ibid:104). The IMF/World Bank, created at the onset of the cold war, but put in abeyance by the Marshal Plan, proved useful at the end of the cold war to create and sustain a "liberal world" through the imposition of special economic and political policies that derive profits for European countries. Through this, the United States and, indeed, the West could act to achieve their economic goals on a concerted basis following what became known as the Washington Consensus.

Dissenting voices in the West questioned the capitalist democracy in the West by those who "denied that what had proven to work best, and afforded the only basis for political legitimacy, was representative democracy based on universal suffrage, within an open, pluralistic society guaranteeing individual freedom... In their questioning, they wanted that there must be freedom not only to inquire and to criticise but to pursue individual advantages within a global market economy" (Noble et al ibid: 1218).

These factors, within a power play of balance of interests, crystallised in a complex fashion towards the end of the cold war, following the collapse of communist Soviet Union, to constitute the doctrine of liberalisation that nourished the basis of SAP, enforced by the Breton Woods institutions. Commissioned by the UN, SAP jolted 38 African countries including Cameroon and marked the Biya government. But this, paradoxically, liberalised the political process but maintained a restriction on the political sphere, leading to popular protests and diverse forms of social conflicts that characterised Cameroon in the early1990s. That further put the nation-building project in jeopardy, nearly destroying the idea as ethno-regional interests overshadowed national interest (see Nyamnjoh 1999).

The creation of state-controlled companies in the immediate post-independence Cameroon, particularly during the developmental period of the 1960s and 1970s, had nothing to do with transforming the invaded territory into a nation. It was a cold war strategy to lure Cameroonians away from communism, which was almost synonymous with the independence struggles that characterised post-war Africa. When the main strand of communism in the Soviet Union, which constituted a kind of international opposition to capitalism was dismantled, there was no need to keep them running. Under the doctrinaire of the neo-liberalism of the late 1980s that signalled the triumph of capitalism under the leadership of the USA, which required a liberal world to launch its economic assault of global dominance. At that point, most of the companies either changed ownership or were simply closed down, leading to the collapse of what was mistakenly supposed to have been Cameroon economy. This opened the way for the introduction of the paradigm for the "fight against poverty" that Cameroonians have become too familiar with.

Since both the political and the economic spheres are inseparable, the liberalisation of the political sphere also meant the liberalisation of the economic sphere. Implementation of World Bank/IMF imposed structural adjustment measures of the late 1980s, lead the way for the adjustment of the structure of Cameroon politics and economy to accommodate foreign companies. This economic restructuring constrained Cameroonians destroying their societies for the enrichment of Europe under arbitrary and anarchical conditions imposed by the UN specialised agencies. While this went on, the individual freedom to inquire and to criticise the political sphere only served to divert attention away from the real issues – the destruction and dehumanisation of the people by foreign organisations in collusion with local government officials.

The emergence of the Social Democratic Front (SDF) in Cameroon could be seen as a product of these forces at play during the end of bi-polarism in Europe, especially following the application of structural adjustment measures that left thousands of Cameroonians jobless. This could explain why it was necessary to prop up the SDF as a new political force in Cameroon, especially after the fall of communism. After the fall of communism, which corresponded to a period of the surfacing of opposition political parties in Africa, the SDF was propped up as a strategy of containing the rising jobless population to keep them busy criticising the government, claiming to offer a social alternative to the assault of capitalism, and yet changing nothing, while the destruction Cameroon went on. Sandrine Lapuyade[17] provides us with one example of the kind of

---

[17] Read Sandrine Lapuyade's "Summary of an Environmental and Social Impact Assessment of CFC operation, April 2000" online at http://www.forestsmonitor/reports/soldownriver/Cameroon.htm accessed in July 2005.

destruction and dehumanisation by foreign companies in collusion with government officials. Legalization of over 200 political parties in Cameroon, after the forceful launching of the SDF on May 26, 1990 left six deaths.

"The Cameroon Forestry Company (CFC) is a subsidiary of the Tharnry France Group. CFC was established in 1990 and operates in Cameroon Eastern Province [region]. Over the last five years, CFC has received numerous favours from the government in contravention of existing legislation ... While it has no legal basis in Cameroon, it has obtained access to far more land for logging than laid down by the law in Cameroon, due to the location of its numerous subsidiaries [its 230] workers living standards does not meet several legal standards [including miserable low wages]".

Most foreign companies that came into Cameroon after the structure of Cameroon's economy had adjusted under SAP did so under misty and very unclear conditions. The agreements reached between them and the government officials were not made public or disclosed to parliament in contravention of the principle of transparency (Jibrin Ibrahim ibid.). This strategy worked well to fulfil the designs of the UN, through its specialised organs, to place Cameroon and 37 other African counties and their people directly under multinationals companies for exploitation and dehumanisation.

This includes initiatives like AGOA, for example, that involved 37 African countries including Cameroon, signed into law by President Bill Clinton on May 18, 2000, and ratified by the USA Congress. It initially intended to last eight years President George W. Bush extended it indefinitely when he signed the AGOA Acceleration Act of July 13, 2004. AGOA successfully kept 37 African countries slaving to rescue the USA economy from decline. While AGOA was a USA initiative to rescue the USA economy from decline, it automatically became international law not only binding on 37 African countries but also subordinating them as appendages of the USA economy within exploitative relations of production. Under AGOA, the USA businessmen were permitted to come in and train those they want to produce what they want for prices determined by them. This is actually in line with the New Deal programme of Paul Biya, to covertly extend USA business into Cameroon by adjusting the structure of Cameroon's economy.

The sale of state corporations, as shown in table 3, also made it possible for the new-imperialism to regain control over [Cameroon] Africa in a deeper and more direct manner than the case for the rest of the developing world (Jibrin Ibrahim ibid.). This situation that the so-called forces of democracy swept across Africa in the 1990s, was just window dressing, could not change. Privatization was just retrieval by the invaders of the economic infrastructure they had acquired during their first invasion of Cameroon since the economy was not nationalised upon "independence." This made the imperial invasion of Cameroon in particular and Africa in general, an uninterrupted process.

Table 4: Trends in the Privatisation of State Corporations

No	Corporation	Year of Privatisation	To	Country of origin
1	C. D. C. Banana Estates	1995	Del Monte	USA
2	SONEL	2002	AES	USA
3	C.D.C Tea Estates	2002	Brobon Finex	South Africa
4	SNEC	-	Suez Lyonnaise des Eaux Group	France
5	CamPost	Feb. 26, 2007	Tescult International Ltd.	Canada
6	REGIFERCAM	2002	Bolloré	France
7	SCB	-	Crédit Lyonnais	France

The trend illustrated in the table above indicates the crying need for a counterpoising political thought to emerge not only in Cameroon but in the whole of Africa. Africa as a continent should have emerged as a dominant bloc to counterbalance such designs and the arrogant destruction of the continent by foreign capital. Instead Africa plays the crying baby, being spoon-fed from outside by European global invaders both directly and through local collaborators. Even the African Union and other sub-regional groupings such as CEMAC, ECOWAS, etc., including states whine. Unfortunately too, the European invaders through the major smoke screens such as the UN, the IMF/World Bank, whose concept of "putting people first" in development programmes as propounded by Michael M. Cernea (ed) (1991), is just part of that grand design aimed at roping in indigenous people to participate in this destruction and enslavement process that is inherent in the globalisation agenda as driven by the European global invaders with local valets and collaborative agencies as accomplices. No reason compels the World Bank/IMF from their offices in New York or Washington D.C, genuinely to concern themselves with attempts at defining the lives of people in communities in Cameroon, and elsewhere in Africa, thousands of miles away, except in the ultimate service of imperial manipulation, dehumanisation, and destruction. Before the birth of the World Bank/ IMF in 1945 these communities existed for thousands of years and will not cease to exist with the disappearance of the UN, IMF/ World Bank, etc.

To justify their concerns and thus interventions, the World Bank (see the World Bank World Development Report 1998/99: *Knowledge for Development*) believes that only industrial countries as opposed to indigenous have the requisite knowledge. The report describes "developing countries", as less knowledgeable and as if they cannot create a social and economic history of their own. Of course, such reports by the World Bank justify the imposition of the Western lopsided development paradigms on the people of Africa as a strategy for subjecting them to exploitation, destruction and enslavement by European counties through programmes such as SAP. Of course, a development paradigm is power in that it has an economic value derived from what it can produce. He who can articulate a development paradigm has power. After having protected their specialised knowledge from spreading, Western countries through the World Bank, since 2003, has involved the production of what it calls Indigenous Knowledge (IK) in *third world* countries. The institution spreads this fabricated IK across societies for free, with no economic benefits for the societies where from such knowledge is derived. This partly helps to hamper the emergence of an alternative development paradigm from Africa. In other words, the production and spread of what is called Indigenous Knowledge (IK) in *third world* countries has no intellectual property rights (IPR) attached. The idea is to pull a fast one on local people – whom they prefer to call development partners. The essence is to ensure that dependent subjects use their own knowledge in slavery to produce for the Western industrial countries under the pretext of poverty alleviation.

To espouse their objectified view of the other as a slave, all research from the West on Africa including those from all the other UN specialised agencies reveals that the intention is only to justify the interventions of the money-grubbing activities and destructive practices of the industrial countries in Africa through their local collaborators. For example, in a booklet entitled *Facts for Life* (February 2002), a joint publication of the UN specialised organs, which is actually an insult on the people of the *third world,* who are presented therein as people who depend on the 'rational' thought of the white man for basic facts of life for their survival. Based on this kind of portrayal of the Other their illegality and imposition on African societies is created and sustained by establishing a category of allegories in themselves which works well for their economic global ventures that ensure the thriving of the global imperial order. This is achieved today through smoke screens called international organisations. The global imperial order wants to be in control of every single idea that crops up in Africa as if those behind it were God who must control African lives in all domains. However, the global imperial order understands the philosophy of chain operation or partnership and so always strives to see the thriving of internal factors that support their activities on the ground.

Internal Factors

The one major thing that needs to be understood in post-colonial studies is that the forces of the global imperial order understands the philosophy of chain operation according to which there must be inside collaborators for its goal to be achieved. The greatest internal factor that has hindered Cameroon from (re)gaining its independence from foreign dictatorship, exploitation, destruction and domination is what can be described as a certain type of blind ambition due to individualistic quest to be "something" by participating in the global criminality perpetrated by the forces of this global imperial order. In South Africa a majority of the population identified racism, slavery and apartheid as the sources of all their evils and so rose up like one man to conquer it, although the Inkatha accepted funding from the white invaders to rival the ANC (Waldemeir 1997: 185). The situation in Cameroon is different. The individualistic quest to benefit from the white man's ill-gotten wealth is overbearing. Yet nobody stops for a moment to ask how European countries got the money they are now fighting to enjoy. How did Western countries get the wealth they now fear to lose?

This situation, which has been going on for decades now yet with no significant impact on the general standards of living, has worked to defeat the national liberation struggle as well as the nation-building project. Monies obtained from international financial agencies through loans or by any means lead not to a generalised capital accumulation through strategic thinking and strategic economic investment for development. Instead the imperialists keep on picking and choosing their local collaborators with whom to exploit and continue with their mission of economic destruction and domination of the Cameroonian masses. This ingratiating political behaviour of betrayal is engrained in the Cameroon political psyche and body politic, from the day the genuine national liberation movement was destroyed in Cameroon and valets foisted on the people. Of course, this has had political consequences of great trepidation. A few examples illustrate this.

As early as 1945 Fouda André placed himself at the service of the French colonial administration that chose him as the unique candidate to be imposed on the nationalist. He was eventually elected to go to the French National Assembly as a representative. When the Cameroonian people elected Douala Manga Bell to argue their case at the UN against the *indégenat*, a form of slavery exercised by the French colonial administration on Cameroonians, upon his return from the UN, he claimed he was answerable to nobody (Wonyu 1985: 236, 237). Douala Manga Bell, who represented France in the UN to give legitimacy to the Trusteeship Agreement as having been endorsed by Cameroonians, is even quoted in the Trusteeship Agreement (p.18) as having told the General Assembly that the document prepaid by France was fit for adoption. Charles Assale, Soppo Priso, etc., who were part of the national liberation movement from the onset soon constituted themselves as institutional mercenaries for the European colonial invaders. Then came André-Marie Mbida, and Jules Ninine who on January 2, 1956 pitched camps in the French National Assembly alongside the French socialist party of French Premier Mollet. This is understandable because anybody in the French colony at that time who proved to think something different from what France was dictating risked losing his life as was the case for André-Marie Mbida. Once appointed Cameroon's first prime minister on May 9, 1957, André-Marie Mbida soon indicated an anti-colonialist leaning. For expressing an anti-colonial leaning, he was dethroned immediately by the French who found a willing horse in Ahmadou Ahidjo who, for his part, naively believed that European invasion and destruction was the best option for Cameroon. This kind of naivety amounted to a betrayal, was possible because of what Joseph (1978:10) says was the excitement to become French citizens at the expense of human liberty.

In West Cameroon, this type of betrayal was also observed. The first generation of the Bakweri people resisted the German invasion, for example, rose up together. The new generation of the Bakweri "educated elite" had imbibed the English language which they considered superior, having gone through the system of Western education. Instead of joining together with their compatriots, these elites distanced themselves from the "illiterate" population and "stood as the official medium of political contact between Southern Cameroons and the British colonial Administration" (Ebune 1992: 125). Quite contrary to expectation, the Bakweri "educated elite" were virtually begging the British for rights and privileges instead of fighting for freedom. Because of Manga Williams's ability to speak good English and his easy associations with whites, the British selected him to sit in the Nigerian Legislative Council wherein he did nothing and represented nobody but put on the mask of Southern Cameroons. In 1959, J.N. Foncha won elections and went to the UN, where he seemed manipulated. Upon his return to Cameroon he dropped his idea of immediate independence and unification and wanted more time for the European stay and exploitation of Cameroon (Mukong 1985: 3). When over 2000 British troops plus 500 police secret agents were deployed in the British trust territory of Cameroon in 1960 as a strategy to isolate that part of Cameroon from the nascent liberation movement, Mbile and Dr. Endeley are accused of having colluded with them in their attempt to falsify the results of the 1961 plebiscite and the 1972 referendum in favour of integration with Nigeria (Zang-Atangana 1989: 199). At the continental level, this phenomenon also held true. Houphouet-Boigny and Sedar Senghor, who were leaders of the inter-territorial nationalist movement, betrayed the struggle by opting to become loyalists to the French socialist party and to gladly sit in the French parliament and draft French laws to be used in repression in equatorial Africa, Algeria, and Vietnam.

Mongo Beti describes this class, which became the *ruling elite,* or better still the local squad of European Governments and International Financial institutions as having become useless and voraciously deceptive in misleading the masses who have blindly followed, pointing out that nationalism and nation-building in Cameroon ended in 1962 with the stroke of President Ahmadou Ahidjo's pen which co-opting Cameroonians into illegality.

> "For the advisers of Ahmadou Ahidjo, the problem was resolved and the battle won around 1962 precisely because, with the elimination of the few politicians who had been still tolerated, repression and terror were used effectively to suppress in embryo any attempt to organise the youth and the urban poor to aid the revolutionaries… This was also the epoch of the explosive blossoming of the ministries, directors, and heads of cabinets, ambassadors, colonels, prefects, and sub prefects, directors of offices of all sorts, president director-generals of national institutions and enterprises … Whoever was not yet "something" believed he would be soon…" (Mongo Beti 1978: 98).

These fireworks of nominations and appointments that Ahmadou Ahidjo's pen generated in 1962 nurtured the basis of this individualistic zest in the citizenry whose attention was now diverted from the course of revolutionary nationalism and nation-building to that of hoping to benefit from an illegal system that was imposed on them by the illegal European invaders. These national bourgeoisie that rose to prominence through nominations and appointments used their immoral status as collaborators of imperialist oppressors to maintain a hegemonic control over the people from top to bottom, thereby compromising the fight for national liberation. Education also played a key role in producing elites who compromised the fight for national liberation. Education tailored from inception to produce mental captives at the service of imperialism, continues to achieve that objective even today.

All of these have impaired visions and deceived the vast majority into believing that the designs and mission of the imperialists to destroy the material base of Africa and to dehumanise its people benefited Africa and its people whose *social becoming* depended on that. These have actually worked against the national liberation struggle and the nation-building project. Subject (not citizens) are more concerned with and are engaged in the process of what Jean-François Bayart describes as the "politics of the belly" rather than in the politics of freedom from foreign invasion and devastation. In any case, this alternative approach to the national liberation struggle could have been beneficial if only the colonial infrastructure was effectively appropriated and used as a weapon against the European invaders themselves in a process that can be said to be that of reverse social engineering. But sadly enough this was not the case since Cameroonians decided to eat bread in slavery than to bake their own bread in freedom. History teaches us that the politics of collaboration with the very people who control the means of adaptation does not pay. The examples of Charles Taylor of Liberia and Pinochet of Chile shed some light on this point. In Liberia, Charles Taylor who offered himself to representatives of the global imperial order in the diamond trafficking enterprise in Liberia later faced charges at The Hague. Pinochet imposed a police state in Chile under the aegis of the USA. The USA used him as a local collaborator to pre-empt the coming to power in Chile of a democratically elected president, Salvador Allende. Pinochet become a prisoner at the international court of justice.

In an address in Senegal on October 2, 2005 President Jacques Chirac of France said Africans were fools to allow themselves to be used, manipulated and killed in this way by imperialists. Though used, manipulated and killed in this way by imperialists, Jacques Chirac said Africans do not seem to have learned a lesson from the experience to start thinking for themselves. The next chapter seeks to point us to where this kind of politics in Cameroon has led Cameroonians.

Chapter Six

The Pitfalls that thwarted the configuration of a nation in Cameroon

The last chapter has demonstrated that as per the political thoughts of the philosophers of the nation in Cameroon, the nation-building project was doomed to fail. This chapter brings out the extent of that failure. We have classified the pitfalls that inadvertently led to the inconclusive termination of the first phase of the national liberation struggle into two main categories – structural and ideological. Structurally, the major political, as well as social and ethnic groupings that emerged in the territory during that period did not all focus on the idea of national liberation. The examples of the Ngondo of the Douala people and the Nkumze of the Bamileke people elucidate this point. Besides these two ethno-social groupings, most of the political formations that emerged in the territory during that period did not all focus on the national liberation struggle. With the national scene characterised by divergent views, the first phase of the national liberation struggle ended prematurely after the direct physical elimination of the nationalist leaders and the obliteration of the national liberation movement by global invaders with local support. Faced with an insurgency, not all Cameroonians saw a threat together against which they would need to all stand. With not all Cameroonians on board the national liberation ship, national liberation and nation building faced an ideological dilemma that in turn fashioned a structural predicament. The inability of Cameroonians to put on one thinking cap as it were in the face of an insurgency because of ideological factors led to a structural aperture. Some of the ideological factors included the systematic putting in place of non-physical but equally violent strategies that were aimed at transforming Cameroonians into lethargic conformists by mutilating their whole state of mental alertness. This category of pitfalls, seem to have completely killed the spirit of national unity and incapacitated the ability of Cameroonians to rationalise action against the global invaders who murdered the cream of the crop who rose up to question the activities of invaders in the territory that eventually became Cameroon.

All political philosophy aims to achieve a political goal. A political philosophy can achieve a political goal for the self only when it originates from the self; not influenced by external forces. It becomes obvious that, even the idea of the Public Service coined by the French for Ahidjo is misleading. That is to say; the putting in place of public service was not Ahmadou Ahidjo's idea to give the self a meaning. The French put in place public service as an ideological mechanism against Cameroonians. Structurally speaking, the inception of the public service in Cameroon had nothing to do with establishing social relations that would build bonds of solidarity among citizens for the satisfaction of the primary needs of the individual citizen based on a political programme with a humanistic content. It had nothing to do with serving the public save for the production and reproduction of the class structure in the post-colony. In other words, the Public Service was instituted in Cameroon to provide a framework for the establishment of structures/institutions to help to coordinate post-colonial activities in Cameroon under the supervision of an unscrupulous, iffy intermediary class of Cameroonians who took over from the Europeans with no other intention than to prepare Cameroon into a capital reprocessing geo-political entity for Western industrial economies. Public Service had more to do with state formation than with nation-building. It served to orientate thinking and to entice Cameroonians into illegality so they could participate in this criminality. The public service played a major function in regrouping Cameroonians into social categories, classes or public spheres. At the immediate post-reunification era in Cameroon, the overbearing influence of the public service led to moral decadence and depravation. Moral decadence and depravation in turn justified the subjugation and domination of post-colonial subjects by global invaders who have moulded and perpetuated perceptions about their own superiority, which eventually destroyed the roots of a home-grown political philosophy in Cameroon.

The rise of this intermediary merchant class of blacks who, by their narcissism sold the governed to the representatives of the global hegemonic order, therefore, had nothing to do with transforming the post-colony into a self-governing entity. Their existence reinforces post-colonial activities for the total destruction of the post-colony under a power structure that manipulates both the emotive and cognitive variables to achieve the goal of postcolonity. Worse still, the narcissism of this intermediary merchant class of blacks who opted to assist the Europeans in instituting postcolonity, have been catastrophic with Cameroonians stumbling from the brink of one tragedy to another. Cameroon has great strategic value to the French invaders. Um Nyobe and the UPC revolution could not have been allowed to succeed for the spill over effect in the entire sub region could have spelled doom for France. If Um Nyobe had succeeded, Cameroon would have been the only country in Black Africa to have won its freedom through a revolution. The rest of the African post-colonial power exchanges have been by power changing hands between the white invaders and those who grew from within their ranks.

Nationalist elsewhere like Kwame Nkrumah and Jomo Kenyatta opted for collaboration with the preposterous representatives of the global imperial order, with Nkrumah winning a peace award in 1954 as a result. These failed to disentangle their respective countries from European invasion, conquest, domination, and destruction, though Kenya and Ghana are apparently doing better than Cameroon economically and politically speaking. Whatever the case, it should be noted that the Ghanaian leadership applied forceful strategies that successfully turned the Ghanaian economy around with Ghana achieving an economic miracle in the 2000s, according to Eboe

Hutchful (2002). This is opposed to Cameroon that instead emerged in the 2000s as a heavily indebted poor country as evaluated by the Breton woods institutions. In any case, awards such as Nkrumah's peace award were intended to pacify the supporters of independence. To Nkrumah, that did not make any difference. For those who took it to heart such as JN Foncha, the devastating consequences are there today though dissimilar in different African countries. Nevertheless, a great deal of the pitfalls that contributed to the failure of the first phase of the national liberation struggle were multidimensional in nature and worked in a way that is unsuspecting to the victims who have been subjected under the supremacy of the global imperial order especially in a world where all the aspects of human life are being subjected entirely to the logic of the market. Subjecting all the aspects of human life entirely to the logic of the market makes Africans, who opted for dependence rather than freedom, not only great losers in the global market economy but are gradually heading towards a catastrophe. As great losers in the global market economy, Cameroonians face economic asphyxiation under the invisible hand of global predators that control the global variables on which Cameroonians depend.

Whether we call it globalisation, modernisation, or whatever heading we may choose to call it, what is important in the political life of a social entity is that it should, at least, be governed by a political philosophy that originated from the people themselves as they struggle to recreate themselves and to control the outcome of their self-recreated image for their own future with minimum external manipulations. This, at least will ensure that the total inputs at any one time are always equal to total outputs. Otherwise the outcome of the "global village" as its proponents gleefully propound can only spell disaster for a majority of individuals who are deprived of this fundamental right within a vague global village that has no village chief so to speak. Benefits of globalisation cannot be overstated if properly harnessed and channelled through a give and take process.

A nation develops as a phalanx, governed by a broad-based ideology that embodies all the individuals within it in all their innermost hopes as they struggle to recreate their future totally under their control, existing *suis generis,* relating with the outside world by way of interdependence and not by dependence. When a nation develops as a phalanx, governed by a broad-based ideology that embodies all the individuals within it and is existing *suis generis,* its citizens will have the freedom to cho0se what elements to incorporate and what not to with total inputs always equal to total outputs. Unfortunately, Cameroon developed as a place of work; a place where people go to find work or do business and to return "home". Regrettably too, since the concept of globalisation became en vogue, with the advent of the "nation-state", the tendency has been to groom a few advocates who sermonize the vague dimensions of globalisation without telling their followers why a nation should development as a weak entity; weak people, and a weak ideology, unable to protect and reproduce itself, with no internal identity of its own, yet hyper-militarised and one-directional, depending on other countries.

Previous chapters demonstrated that for the past decades nation-building in Cameroon primarily benefited the so-called elite and the educated class as well as the rest of the post-colonial thinkers, blind followers, trapped in the unidirectional ideological mind-set of global invaders. This was made possible by the introduction of ideological tools that were intended to facilitate the agenda of global invasion, which has been re-baptised under a subtlety called globalisation. Cameroon emerged as a nation-state out of the criminal practices of these global invaders. Valets of global invaders have governed Cameroon with unidirectional mindedness compelled to develop both theory and methodology. The objective of converting Cameroonians into vague global citizens gave no consideration to the development of a nation that is self-transformational. This has given birth to a non-existent nation (a statist state) held together by a complex combination of class and ethnic differences, producing an identity that derives from differential disarray or from a degree of discrepancy.

To avoid the trappings that led to this differential disarray, it would be absolutely necessary, in this second phase of the national liberation struggle, which must be aimed at Cameroonians recovering the totality of their being, for Cameroonians to transform themselves into men and women who can neither be bought nor sold. This is especially germane within a global context of invisible and ubiquitous undercurrents that influence every single department of life, making the money chase seeming to be the only index of success, which in turn has tended to make self-organisation and self-determination impossible. With regards to education, the new nationalism must see beyond the monumental ineptitudes of the educated class and their pro-modernist followers in whose brainwashed mind-set education has been reduced to mean only literacy, with no reference to the self. With education seen only as the means through which to gain and lead a good life, intellectuals who ought to have served as the vanguard building anti-imperialists national consciousness have become mercenaries at the expense of freedom. Hence, the broad dimensions that should define for us the national liberation struggle, which should centre around the key issue of ending European invasion, domination, and the destruction of our societies, was narrowed only to mean the struggle by the "native" to control the material resources or to grab money. By pleading with the European invading conquerors to improve on their relationship with the colonised peoples the new loyalist nationalists compromised the national liberation struggle. This must be redefined to mean the complete renewal of the mind and then reprogramming it with sound knowledge of the self for the emergence of a completely new society from the ashes of the present dispensation.

Once again Cameroon's tragic mishap began with the brutal murder of Um Nyobe, the symbol of the Cameroon national liberation struggle, by the French with local assistance. This crime destroyed the nascent national consciousness that would have embraced the various social strata and political forces in Cameroon in all their hopes and serve as a forum for mobilizing Cameroonians against Europeans without necessarily "detribalising" as Um Nyobe had maintained. This crime also trapped Cameroonians into droopy, apathetic searchers of money and pleasure-seekers within an externally supported state system. Having succeeded through the support of European valets, nation-building in Cameroon gave the wrong impression of the existence of a national pie or that of an elephant state as Zambo Belinga puts it. Cameroonians came away with the wrong impression following the emergence of the post-colonial state when the economy seemingly flourished under French planning and direction. French economic interest was actually that there was a national pie that has to be shared and that this sharing was the end results of political action Zambo Belinga (1997). This wrong impression Cameroonians came away with following the advent of the post-colonial state in Cameroon can be testified to by the number of state bureaucrats incarcerated following accusations of stealing public money. The incarceration of public servants signifies that life in the post-colony has come to mean only the struggle for money and the quest to acquire and surround oneself with material wealth rather than the continuous creation and recreation of the future from the debris of the past. Caught up in this runaway struggle for money and the quest to acquire and surround oneself with material wealth, many have become mercenaries within the national and international racket system (cf. Cornea 1991: 36). Yet life is worth much more than just the search for money and material accumulation, which are fleeting illusions. Life is a continuous creation and recreation of the future from the debris of the past in constant search for eternal beauty by way of conquest and symbolic objectification of the divide between the spiritual and the material (cf. Soyinka 1976).

The ideological tools adopted within the post-colonial context clearly reveal the blunders of the past that marred the nation-building project in Cameroon and set in motion a process of retrogression eventually giving birth to a country with an identity that derives from differential disarray or from a degree of an un-bargained discrepancy.

Since then the tactics of the imperialist have consisted mainly of continuously alienating the people from their means of self-reorganisation and self-preservation, with the youths as main victims. Our youth are constantly deceived and disconnected from their Ancestral roots which link them to the real world of nature-culture interaction where their future should depend. This prevents the youths from recreating their future from their decomposed, abysmal past but to keep on recreating neo-Europes at their own peril and at the expense of a strong and efficient nation that is capable of empowering its citizens to respond to their immediate needs.

The remaking of the post-coly must go beyond the petty issues of seeking to improve relations with imperial nations to actually focussing on what they are and have that can be given to the world as a contribution to the development of the global culture. Having said that, let us now look at what really happened after the premature end of the first phase of the national liberation struggle. This should guide action during the second phase of the national liberation struggle towards the attainment of national independence, comprising of independence of thought and independence of action.

The emergence of an Ideological state apparatus in lieu of a nation

In the course of this work, it has been discovered that what is commonly referred to as a nation in Cameroon is actually an ideological state apparatus that was created in lieu of a nation.

Cameroon is not a social system by any standards because it lacks the three key ideas that characterises a system. Cameroon is neither a system of transformation preserved and enriched by its own transformation laws nor an auto-regulating complex whole and therefore not a structural whole. The key issue that constituted the foundation philosophy of Cameroon was not about creating a self-regulating, self-transformational totality. Instead the key issue was to create an open field for European economic interests. The unconvincing banalities about the indispensability of foreign partners or foreign currency leaves the impression that if something were to happen, mysteriously, and all the global imperial order disappear, the logical outcome would be that Cameroon would automatically cease to exist since the latter is inexorably linked to the former, which constitutes its source of existence.

Another of looking at Cameroon as a non-social system regards the equilibrium of systems as they adapt to their environments. For a social system to maintain itself at equilibrium, in relation to other social systems, the forces acting inside the system must be equal to the forces acting outside it. In Newtonian terms, the forces acting in a system must be equal and opposite to those acting outside it. In other words, if the total input is more than the total output this may lead to an imbalance or a disequilibrium that can lead to a deformation on the system and could negatively affect its contents. This is exactly the case in Cameroon. However, although a mechanical system is different from a social system in that a social system can be enriched by discretionally borrowing foreign elements, which constitutes its input. Nevertheless, a social system does not depend entirely on a foreign element, yielding results external to it. Furthermore, a social system is comprised of human beings who know what they want or know what is good for them hence do not need to be forced, persuaded or convinced or even told (by forces from outside) what to think or do since human beings are capable of recognising, borrowing, and integrating into their system in an innovative manner what they think can lead to the enrichment of their social system for their well-being within the potency of the springs and capacitors of the social system itself.

Therefore, consistent with a theory developed by Louis Althusser (1971), Cameroon is an ideological state apparatus and not a nation. Just for clarity sake, while the term ideology refers to that invisible storehouse of ideas or a pool from where people in a particular social milieu draw the common sense notions for their daily living, an ideological state apparatus is a state that serves an ideological purpose; a purpose that may be totally inconsistent with the real interest of its people. Differently stated, an ideological state apparatus is that high realm of political power put in place to achieve an ideological goal such as controlling thought among the governed thus deploying all pedagogic techniques in ensuring that the governed belong to a particular ideological leaning only, with no alternative. Following his long years of research amongst the ancient nations of the Western Grass fields of West/Central Africa, Jean Pierre Warnier (1975, 1983 concluded that a nation is not created by decrees. Jean Pierre Warnier in fact found out that a nation originates from the free will of a group of people who have decided to go into a social engagement to constitute themselves as the core group around which other social strata will later on be embedding for the growth and development of strata of people into a nation that emerges from that process as a body of one people with one focus. The first stage in the creation of Cameroon was the creation of the office of the president of the republic rather than broad social engagement. Ahmadou Ahidjo appointed by a French governor, Jean Remadier, in February 1958 to replace André Marie Mbida also appointed a year earlier by Pierre Messmer, a French High Commissioner, promulgated into force a draconian law No. 60 PJL-ANF of 1963, which practically destroyed the foundation of the nation. This law abolished all groups and associations and all sheds of opinion in the country and brought Cameroon under a state of emergency. This decree put an end to the thinking capacity of all Cameroonians and by implication rendered Cameroonians inert. It basically stopped them from engaging in any sort of activity that emanated from their own thought process.

With all powers in the country vested in the office of the President of the Republic and its antennas, notably the CNU party, and all the instruments of state power such as the army, gendarmerie, and the Military Tribunals, the putting in place of an ideological state apparatus in lieu of a nation was a forgone conclusion. With Cameroonians having denied the right to think, the state became the only guarantor of life and property within the territorial boundaries and the only underwriter of foreign protection as President Ahmadou Ahidjo himself puts it in Ahidjo 1964: 24, Ahidjo 1968: 43). Communities and all social strata were expected to abandon all primordial loyalties and submit to the imposing will of the European superimposed secular state which they must look up to as the giver and guarantor of life. At this point in time, President Ahmadou Ahidjo, put in place post-colonial institution including ministerial departments and other government services and after putting in place the *Ecole Nationale d'Administration et de Magistrature,* (ENAM), *a* professional school, among others, to train those who would guarantee the maintenance and the reproduction of the post-colonial institutions. After he manoeuvred and brought on board the other portion of the territory under British rule in 1961, in 1962 president Ahmadou Ahidjo embarked on what Mongo Beti (1978:98) describes as fireworks of nominations and appointments. These nominations and appointments drew the attention of all Cameroonians, including those of the English speaking extraction, to the state and made persons and local communities to lay their hope on the post-colonial arrangement which has made them to believe that the post-colonial arrangement is truly the guarantor of life and property within the territorial boundaries as well as the underwriter of foreign protection. At this stage, communities and persons began clamouring to gain the favour of the ideological state apparatus for that was the only way they thought they could meet their hopes and expectations in a modern context. Anybody not yet something hoped to be something soon. Yaoundé became the focus of thought. Peripheral communities rejoiced when one of theirs was appointed. That way, the ideological state apparatus did not only succeed in its mission to get Cameroonians on board an ideological leaning with no alternative but actually successfully concocted something called Cameroon into existence. Such a concocted political arrangement cannot be called a nation by any standard but an ideological state apparatus. For this reason, the remaking of the post-colony has been conceived as the struggle to cast off an ideological state apparatus and to reconfiguring the social space into a nation. Um Nyobe/UPC's national liberation struggle was a struggle by the people of Cameroon to liberate themselves from other human beings who had invaded their land and were enslaving them. As far as the second national liberation struggle is concerned, it is a struggle by the people of Cameroon to liberate themselves from a fixation; an ideological state apparatus that controls the mental life of Cameroonian thus determining against the wishes of Cameroonians which direction their lives must take. It is a do or die struggle.

Conclusion

The forgone analyses have shown that following the premature termination of the national liberation movement, Cameroon and Cameroonians became something like orphans in the face of the forces of occupation, which constituted a historical challenge that needed thoughts and actions coordinated in a certain way to overcome it. The premature end of the national liberation movement meant that decolonisation in Cameroon was never pushed to its logical conclusion as a new breed of fake nationalist came upon the scene and did what was totally contrary to what the national liberation movement had set out to achieve. Unlike the rest, Um Nyobe's political philosophy points us to the fact that had he successfully rallied Cameroonians under one stream of political consciousness. Had he successfully pushed the national liberation struggle to its logical end as he had wished, there would have arisen in Cameroon a home-grown ideology that counters the ideology of hegemonic dominance that is actually a menace to the human mind across the globe in modern times. Since that did not happen and an ideological state apparatus emerged in lieu of a nation, the second national liberation struggle should be geared towards casting off an ideological state apparatus. Ridding the people of this ideological straight jacket that perpetuates the ideology of hegemonic dominance is inevitable if Cameroonians are to survive the assault of imperialism covertly targeting the people of Africa.

Bibliography

Ahidjo, A., 1968; La *Pensée Politique d'Ahmadou Ahidjo*. Edition Paul Bory. Monte Carlos.

Ahidjo, A., 1974; *Contribution à la construction nationale*. Présence Africaine. Paris.

Ahidjo, A., 1976; *Fondement et Perspectives du Cameroun Nouveau*. Edition Saint-Lambert. Paris.

Aina, T. A., 2003; "Scales of Suffering, Orders of Emancipation: Critical Issues in Democratic Development in Africa", in *African Sociological Review*, 7, 1, 2003 CODESRIA. Dakar.

Ake, C., 1978; *Revolutionary Pressures in Africa*. Zed Press Ltd. London.

Ake, C., 2000; *The Feasibility of Democracy in Africa*. CODESRIA. Dakar.

Amin, A. A., 1997; "The Government Social Policy and National Integration", in Nkwi, P. N., and Nyamnjoh, F. B., (eds.) *Regional Balance and National Integration in Cameroon: Lessons Learned and the Uncertain Future*. ICASSRT Monograph 1. Yaoundé.

Anderson, B., 1983; *Imagined Communities: Reflections on the Origin and Spread of Nationalism*. Verso. London and New York.

Ardener E., and Ardener S., 1960; *Plantation and Village in the Cameroons*. Oxford University, Press. Oxford.

Ardener S., (ed), 2003; *Swedish Ventures in Cameroon 1883 – 1923: Trade and Travel, People and Politics*. Bergham Book. New York. Oxford.

Aschroft, B., Griffiths G., and Tiffins, H., (eds), 1995; *The Post-Colonial reader*, Routledge, London.

Bandolo, H., 1985; *La Flamme et La Fumée* Editions SOPECAM Yaounde.

Bishop, Alan, J. 1990; 'Western Mathematics: The Secret Weapon of Cultural Imperialism', *Raceand* Class 32 (2): 51-65.

Biya P., *Anthologie de discours et Interviews de Président de la République de Cameroun 1982-2002*. Editions SOPECAM. Yaoundé

Biya, P., 1986; *Communal Liberalism*. Macmillan. London.

Bourdieu, P., 1994; *Raisons Pratiques: Sur la théorie de l'action*. Editions du Seuil. Paris

Calvocoressi, P., 1985; *World Politics Since 1945*. Second Edition. Longman. London.

Césaire, Aimé, 1946 ; *Et les chaines se taisaient*, in *Les Armes Miraculeuses*, Gallimard. Paris.

Cernea, Michael M., (ed), 1991; *Putting People First: Sociological Variables in Rural Development*. A World Bank Publication, Second Edition. Oxford University Press. Oxford.

Chaffard, G., 1967; *Les Carnets secrets de décolonisation*, vol. II. Calman-Levy. Paris.

Chia, E. N., (ed), 2006; *African Linguistics and the development of African communities*. CODESRIA. Dakar.

Clignet, R., 1980; "The multiplicity of Times in the Cameroonian Modern Labour Force", in Ndiva Kofele-Kale (ed.), *An African Experiment in Nation-Building: The Bilingual Cameroon Republic since Reunification*. Westview Press. Colorado.

Courade, G., 1997; "La Creation du Territoire National Camerounais a l' éxpreuve de crise et de sa Gestion", in Nkwi, P. N., and Nyamnjoh, F. B., (eds.), *Regional Balance and National Integration in Cameroon: Lessons Learned and the Uncertain Future*. ICASSRT Monograph 1. Yaounde.

Crosby, A.W., 1986; *Ecological Imperialism: The Biological Expansion of Europe 900 -1900*. Cambridge University Press. Cambridge.

Davidson, D., 1994; *Modern Africa: A Social and Political History*. Third Edition. Longman. London.

Dumont, René, 1962; *L'Afrique Noire est mal partie*, Seuil. Paris

Dumont, R. et Mattin, M-F, 1982; *L'Afrique Etranglée*. Editions du Seuil. Paris.

Eboua, S., 1985 ; *Ahidjo et la logique du pouvoir*. L'Harmattan. Paris.

Ebune, J. B, 1992; *The Growth of Political Parties in Southern Cameroons 1916-1960* CEPER, Yaounde.

Eleih-Elle E., 1993; *Renouveau Ou es Tu.* Beijing.

Engels, F., 1979 (Translated) "The History of Primitive Christianity" in *Pre-Capitalist Socio-Economic Formation: A collection.* Progress publishers. Moscow

Escobar, A., 1995; *Encountering Development: The Making and Unmaking of the Third World.* Princeton University Press. Princeton.

Eteki-Otabela, M.–.L., 1987; *Misere et Grandeur de la Democratie au Cameroun.* L'Harmattan. Paris.

Eyinga A., 19878; *Mandate d'Arrete: Pour Cause d'Election: De la Democratie au Cameroun.* Editions L'Harmattan

Fame Ndongo, J., 19 *Le Prince et le Scribe: Lecture Politique et esthétique du Roman négro-africain Post-colonial.* Berger – Levrault. Paris.

Fanon F., 1967; *The Wretched of the Earth.* The Chaucer Press Ltd. Suffolk

Fogui, J.-.P., 1990; *L'Intégration Politique au Cameroun: une Analyse Centre périphérie.* I.G.D.J. Paris.

Foucault, M., 1970; *The Other of Things: An Archaeology of Human Sciences.* New York.

Foucault, M., 1988; "The Ethic of Care of the Self as a Practice of Freedom", in *The Final Foucault,* eds J. Bernauer and D. Rasmussen, MIT Press. Cambridge.

Freund, Bill, 1984; *The Making of Contemporary Africa: The Development of African Society since 1800.* Macmillan Press Ltd. London.

Geisler, W, 1994, *AIDS: Origin, Spread and Healing* (shortened Version) Marianum Press, Kisubi.

Guiffo, S.L, 1993; *Challenge Hebdo et le Patriote dans la Transition Démocratique au Cameroun : Deux Approche du Traitement de l'Information Politique Nationale du 1er Octobre 1990 au 31 Octobre 1992.* DSSTIC dissertation, ASMAC/ESSTIC Yaounde (Mimeograph).

Gwellem, J.F., 1984; *Paul Biya, Hero of the New Deal.* Limbe.

Hattemer, B., 1996; "Cause and Violent Effect: Media and Our Youth", in Joan Gorham(ed) *Mass Media: Annual Editions*

96/97. Dushkin Publishing Group/Brown and Benchmark Publishers, Sluice Dock, Connecticut06437.

Hattemer, B., and Showers, H.R., 1993; *Don't Touch that Dial: The Impact of the Media on Children and the Family*. Huntington House.

Hargreaves, J.D., 1996; *Decolonisation in Africa*. Second Edition. Longman. London

Hendricks, C., and Mandala, 2002; "Beggars Can't be Choosers: Reflections on the Zimbabwe Quagmire", in CODESRIA Bulletin No. 1 & 2 PP. 9-11

Hendricks, F., 2002 "Inter-personal Racism after Apartheid", in CODESRIA Bulletin No 1 & 2, PP. 3-8

Hobsbawm, E., and Terence Ranger (eds), 1983; *The Invention of Tradition*. Cambridge University Press. Cambridge

James, G.M., 1992; *Stolen Legacy: Greek Philosophy is Stolen Egyptian Philosophy*. Africa Press World Press, Trenton, New Jersey.

Jibrim Ibrahim, 2002; "Notes on Globalisation and the Marginalisation of Africa," in CODESRIA Bulletin, Special issue No. 3 & 4, 2002. Dakar.

Johnson, W. R., 1970; *The Cameroon Federation: Political Integration in a Fragmentary Society*. Princeton University Press. Princeton.

Joseph, R., 1986 ; Le Mouvement Nationaliste Au Cameroun : *Les Origines Sociale de L'UPC*.

Editions Karthala. Paris.

Joseph, R. A, 1978; *Gaullist Africa: Cameroon under Ahmadou Ahidjo*. Fourth Dimension Publishers Enugu,

Joseph, R. A., 1974; "Ruben Um Nyobe and the 'Kamerun' Rebellion", in *African Affairs: Journal of the Royal African Society*, Vol. 73. No 293 PP 428-443 Oct. 1974. Oxford University Press. Oxford.

Kengne Fodouop, 1997; "Elite et Integration National au Cameroon sous le Régime du renouveau", in Nkwi, P. N., and Nyamnjoh, F. B., (eds.), *Regional Balance and National Integration in Cameroon: Lessons Learned and the Uncertain Future*. ICASSRT Monograph 1. Yaounde.

Kengne Pokam, 1980; *La religion face au pouvoir politique au Cameroun, thèse de doctorat d'Etat en sciences politique*, Poitiers.

Kengne Pokam, 1986; *La Problématique de L'unité national au Ca*meroun. Editions l'Harmattan. Paris.

Kengne Pokam, 1987; *Les églises chrétiens face á la montée du nationalisme Camerounais.* Points De Vue, L'Harmattan. Paris.

Keohane, R.O.; Nye, J.S.; Hoffman, S. (eds.), 1993; *After the Cold War: International Institutions and State Strategies in Europe, 1989-1991.*HarvardUniversity Press. Massachusetts.

Kiawi, E. C., and Mfoulou, J., 2002, "Rethinking African Development: Social Science Perspective", in CODERIA Bulletin No. 1 & 2 PP. 12-17

Konde, E., 1998; *The Bassa of Cameroon: An Indigenous African Democracy Confronts European Colonisation.* Tapestry Press Ltd. Acton.

Konings, P., and Nyamnjoh, F.B., 2003 *Negotiating and Anglophone Identity. A Study of the Politics of Recognition and Representation in Cameroon.* Brill, Leiden

Kuoh, C. -.T, 1992; *Le Cameroun de l'après-Ahidjo (1970-1982).* Karthala. Paris.

Kwame Nkrumah, 1964; *Consciencism.* Panaf Books. London.

Le Vine V. T., 1964; *Cameroon: From Mandate to Independence.* University of California Press. Berkeley.

Levi-Strauss, C., 1972; *The Savage Mind* Weidenfeld & Nicolson. London

Levi-Strauss, C., 1983; *Le Regard Éloigné.* Librairie Plon. Paris.

Lewis, Gordon, 1978; *Slavery, Imperialism, and Freedom: Studies in English Radical Thought.* Monthly Review Press. New York and London.

Mbembe, A., 1984*; Le Problem Nationale Kamerunais*. l'Harmattan. Paris.

Mbembe, A., 1992; "Provisional Notes on the Post-Colony", *Africa,* 62 (1).

Mbembe, A., 1996; *La naissance du maquis dans le Sud-Cameroun (1920 – 1960) ; Histories des usages de la raison en colonies.* Karthala. Paris.

Mbock, C. B., 1985; *Cameroun: L'Intention Democratique.* Editions SOPECAM. Yaoundé.

Memmi, Albert, 1965; *The Coloniser and the Colonised.* Orion. New York

Mende, Tibor, 1973; *From Aid to Recolonisation: Lessons of a Failure.* Pantheon. New York

Mongo Beti; 1984; *Main Base sur le Cameroun.* Editions des peoples Noirs. Rouen.

Mongo Beti, 1986; *Lettres Ouverte aux Camerounais ou la deuxième mort de Ruben Um Nyobe.* Editions de Peuples Noirs. Rouen.

Mongo Beti, 1993; *La France Contre l'Afrique retour au Cameroun.* La Decouverte. Paris.

Morin, Edgar, 1994; *Sociology.* Payard. Paris

Mukong, A. W., 1985; *Prisoner without a Crime.* Alfresco. Limbe.

Mveng, E., 1985; "Is There a Cameroon Culture?" in *The Cultural Identity of Cameroon.* Ministry of Information Culture. Yaounde.

Mzeka, 1980; *The Core Culture of Nso*, Jerome Radin Co., USA.

Nash, A., 2003; "Third Worldism", in *African Sociological Review*, 7, 1, 2003, pp. 94-116 CODESRIA. Dakar.

Ndiva Kofele-Kale (ed), 1980; *An African Experiment in Nation-Building: The Bilingual Cameroon Republic Since Reunification.* Westview Press. Colorado.

Ndongko, T.M, and Tambo, I.L., 2000; *Educational Development 1961 – 1999: Issues and Perspectives.*Nkemnji Global Tech. USA

Ndzana, M.H., 1985; *L'Idée sociale chez Paul Biya.* Université de Yaounde. Yaounde

Nga Ndongo, V., 1993; *Les Medias au Cameroun: Mythes et désires d'une société en crise.* Edition l'Harmattan. Paris.

Ngayap, P. F., 1983; *Cameroun: Qui gouverne? De Ahidjo à Biya, L'héritage et L'enjeu* l'Harmattan. Paris.

Ngoh, V. J., (ed), 2004; *Cameroon: From Federal to Unitary State 1961 - 1972.* Design House. Limbe.

Ngwana, S. A., 2003; *Population and Development.* African Development Corporation Ltd. Douala.

Ngwasiri, C. N., 1997; "The Effectiveness of Legal Instruments in Achieving Regional Balance and National Integration in Cameroon", in Nkwi, P. N., and Nyamnjoh, F. B.,(eds.), *Regional Balance and National Integration in Cameroon: Lessons Learned and the Uncertain Future.* ICASSRT Monograph 1. Yaounde.

Nkwi, N. & Warnier, J.P., 1982; *Elements for a History of the Western Grassfields,* University of Yaounde. Yaounde.

Nkwi, N.P; 1989; *The German Presence in the Western Grassfields 1891-1913: A German Colonial Account.* Leiden.

Nkwi, P.N, 1986; *Traditional Diplomacy: A Study of the Inter-chiefdom Relations in the Western Grassfields, North West Province of Cameroon.* Yaounde: Publications of the Department of Sociology, University of Yaounde. Yaounde.

Nkwi, P.N., 1976; *Traditional Government and Social Change. A Study of the Political Institutions among the Kom of the Cameroon Grassfields.* The University Press. Studia Ethnographica Friburgensia. Fribourg.

Northern, T., 1979; *Splendour and Secrecy, Art in the Cameroon Grassland. Page Primitive and Ancient Art.* New York.

Ntumazah, N., 2001; *A Conversational Autobiography.* Patron Publishing House. Bamenda.

Nyamnjoh, F.B., 1996; Mass *Media and Democratisation in Cameroon.* Friedrich Ebert Stiftung. Yaounde.

Nyamnjoh, F.B., 1999; "Cameroon: A Country United by Ethnic Ambitions and Difference" in *African Affairs": The Journal of the Royal African Society.*Vol 98 No 390 PP. 101-118 Jan. 1999. Oxford University Press. Oxford.

Le Renouveau Camerounais; Certitudes et défis: Essai sur les douze premiers mois de Paul Biya, 1983; Par un Groupe de Citoyens. Editions ESSTI, Université de Yaoundé. Yaoundé.

Ombe Ndzana, V., 1987; *Agriculture, pétrole et politique au Cameroun: Sortie de la crise?* L'Harmattan, Paris

Piaget, J., 1970; *Structuralism.* Basic Books Inc., New York.

Roberts, S.H., 1963; *The History of French Colonial Policy 1970-1925.* Frank Cass and Co. Ltd. London.

Rodney, W., 1972; *How Europe Underdeveloped Africa*, Bogle-L'Ouverture Publications. London

Rudin, R., 1958; *The Germans in the Cameroons, 1884-1914*. YaleUniversity Press. New Haven.

Samir Amin, 1977; *Imperialism and Unequal Development*. Monthly Review Press. New York.

Samir Amin, 1994; *Re-Reading the Post war Period. An Intellectual Itinerary*. Monthly Review Press. New York.

Serequeberhan, T., 2002; "The Critique of Eurocentrism and the Practice of African Philosophy", in Coetzee, P.A and Roux, A.P.J. (eds.) [2002]; *Philosophy from Africa*. Oxford University Press, Cape Town.

Smith, A. D., 1996, "State-Making and Nation-Building", in J.A. Hall (ed) *States in History*. Basel Blackwell. PP. 228-6) Oxford

Spengler, Oswald [1926] 1962; *The Decline of the West*. Random House 1962. New York.

Stallcup, K, 1974; "Geographie Linguistique des Grassfields", in HYMAN and VOEHOEVE (ed.) Symposium on Patterns in Languages and Society: Sub-Saharan Africa". 6th Conference on African Linguistics. Columbus: Ohio.

Tambo, L.I., 2003; *Principles and Methods of Teaching: Applications in Cameroon Schools*. Anucam Publishers.

Tardits, C., 1980; *Le Royaume Bamoun*, Librairie Armand Collin. Paris.

Tita Nji, V; Gwanfogbe, M.; Nwana; Ndangam; Lima, A.S., 1988; *An Introduction to the Study of Bali Nyonga: Tribute to His Royal Highness Galea II, Trditional Ruler of Bali-Nyonga from 1940 – 1985*. Stardist Printers. Yaounde.

Touraine, A, 1965; *Sociologie de L'Action*. Editions du Seuil. Paris.

Su Aaron, 1991; *Nationalism and Nation-Building in Africa*. Baseria-Publications, Basel.

Tanjong, Enoh, 2006; *Africa in international Communication*. Design House Limbe.

Tanjutek, 1998; *The 500 Years Curse: 1492-1992*. P.T. Pacodana Indoexim Abadi. Singapore.

Touraine, Alain, 1974; Pour *La Sociologies* Editions du Seuil. Paris.

Um Nyobe R., *Unification Immédiate du Cameroun,* Intervention de Um Nyobe au Congrés de Kumba 14 – 17 December 1951, Imprimerie Spécial des étudiants Camerounais.

Um Nyobe, *Ce que veut le people Camerounais* (Comité Directeur de l'UPC. 1952).

Um Nyobe, "Naissance du mouvement national au Cameroun", *Cahiers Internationaux,* no. 52 (Janvier 1954), PP. 78 – 82.

Um Nyobe, "Objective immédiate du mouvement national Camerounais", *Cahiers Internationaux,* no. 53 (Février 1954), PP. 75 – 80.

Um Nyobe, "Où est le nationalisme Camerounais ?", *Cahiers Internationaux,* no.64 (Mars 1955), PP.81- 80.

UM Nyobe, "Profession de Fois du Candidat Ruben Um Nyobe au Election Législative du 17 Juin 1951.

Um Nyobe, "Rapport de Dschang", Présenté au Premier Congrès de l'UPC à Dschang le 10

Avril 50 par Um Nyobe, Vice-Président de RDA, Secrétaire Général de L'UPC.

Um Nyobe, 1957; *Les vraies solutions pour une détente politique et morale au Cameroun,* Inter- Compos. Montmartre. Paris.

Um Nyobe, 1961; *La Pensée de Um Nyobe.* Bureau Provisoire de l'UPC. Yaounde.

van den Berg, A., 1997; "Women between Chiefs and the Law: Competition for Power and Land in North Cameroon", in Nkwi, P. N., and Nyamnjoh, F. B., (eds.), *Regional Balance and National Integration in Cameroon: Lessons Learned and the Uncertain Future.* ICASSRT Monograph 1. Yaoundé.

Van den Berghe, Pierre L., 1967; *Race and Racism: A contemporary Perspective.* John Wiley. New York.

Waldmeir, P., 1997; *Anatomy of a Miracle: The End of Apartheid and the Birth of the New South Africa.* W.W. Norton and Company. New York. London.

Warnier, J.P., 1975; *Precolonial Mankon: The Development of a Cameroon Chiefdom in its Regional Setting.* Ph.D. Thesis University of Pennsylvania.

Warnier, J.-P., 1983; *Sociologie du Bamenda Pre-colonial (Cameroun)*. Thèse présentée en vue du grade de docteur ès lettres. Université de Paris X.

Warnier, J.-P., 1984; "The History of the Peopling of Western Cameroon and the Genesis of its Landscape", *Journal of African History*, 25:395 – 410.

Warnier, J.P., 1985; *Echanges, développement et hiérarchies dans le Bamenda Précolonial (Cameroon)*. Stuttgart: Franz Sterner Verlag 76.

Wole Soyinka, 1976; *Myth, Literature and the African World*. Cambridge University Press. Cambridge.

Wonyu II, N.-.L., 1988; *Cameroun: Plaidoyer Pour le Patriote Martyre: Um Nyobe* l'Harmattan. Paris

Wonyu, E., 1985; *Cameroun: De L'UPC A L'UC.: temoignage à l'aube de l'independence (1953-1961)*. L'Harmattan. Paris

World Bank Report, 1997; *Private Capital Flows to Developing Countries: The Road to Financial Integration*. ISBN 0-19-521116-2.

World Bank, 1995, *Workers in an Integrating World*. World Development Report 1996 ISBN 0-19-521103-0.

World Bank, 1996, *From Plan to Market*. World Development Report 1996. ISBN 0-19-521107-3.

World Bank, World Development Report 1998/99: *Knowledge for Development*. Oxford University Press. Oxford

Woungly–Massaga, 1984; *Ou va le Kamerun?* l'Harmattan. Paris.

Yenshu Vubo, E. and Ngwa, G.A., 2001; "Changing Intercommunity Relations and the Politics of Identity in the Northern Mezam Area, Cameroon", *Cahiers d' Etudes Africaines*, 161, XLI – 1, 2001 PP. 163 – 190.

Yenshu, Vubo, E., 2001; *Itinerant Craftsmen, Highland Farmers and Royal Herdsmen: An Interpretation of Kejom Historical Traditions*. Design House. Limbe.

Zambo Belinga, J. M., "Equilibre Regional, Replis identitaire et Fragilisation Croisante de l'Interet National: Vers un Effect "boomerang" de la Politique des Quotas au Cameroun", in Nkwi, P. N., and Nyamnjoh, F. B.,(eds.), *Regional Balance and*

National Integration in Cameroon: Lessons Learned and the Uncertain Future. ICASSRT Monograph 1. Yaounde.

Zang-Atangana, J- M, 1989; *Les Forces Politique au Cameroun Unifie.* (Tome Premier). *Les parties politiques avant la réunification.* Éditions l'Harmattan. Paris

Zeleza, T. P., 1997; *Manufacturing African Studies,* CODESRIA. Dakar.

¹⁴ For a clearer view on how priority was given to food production in the pre-colonial states in which everybody was involved in the process of production, including even the Head of State and all other things were secondary, especially in the particular case of the pre-colonial Cameroon Western Grassfields states, see my *a communal political system: a case of classical African political systems*

www.ingramcontent.com/pod-product-compliance
Lightning Source LLC
Chambersburg PA
CBHW070831300426
44111CB00014B/2516